H21 790 977 6   SYLVESTER, D.   A history of
                                  Gwynedd
          AS 7/87   8.95

942.92   7/12

HERTFORDSHIRE LIBRARY SERVICE
                                    e the
                                    enewed

45 901 339 4

L.32/rev.81

Hertfordshire

942.
92
SYL

1 2 JUN 2010

Please renew/return this item by the last date shown.

So that your telephone call is charged at local rate,
please call the numbers as set out below:

	From Area codes 01923 or 020:	From the rest of Herts:
Renewals:	01923 471373	01438 737373
Enquiries:	01923 471333	01438 737333
Textphone:	01923 471599	01438 737599

L32   www.hertsdirect.org/librarycatalogue

D1346423

A HISTORY OF GWYNEDD

(Anglesey, Caernarvonshire, Merioneth)

Senate House of Owain Glyn Dŵr, Dolgellau.

THE DARWEN COUNTY HISTORY SERIES

A History of Gwynedd

(Anglesey, Caernarvonshire, Merioneth)

DOROTHY SYLVESTER

Drawings by Grace Corbett

Cartography by James Hogan ·

PHILLIMORE

1983

Published by
PHILLIMORE & CO. LTD.
Shopwyke Hall, Chichester, Sussex

© Dorothy Sylvester, 1983

ISBN 0 85033 477 2

HERTFORDSHIRE
LIBRARY SERVICE

Printed in Great Britain by
BIDDLES LTD.
Guildford, Surrey

and bound by
THE NEWDIGATE PRESS LTD.
Dorking, Surrey

Contents

Maps

Plates

Preface

In 1974, the three north-western counties of Wales were united to form a new county named Gwynedd. Its shape is almost exactly that of the ancient kingdom of that name which for centuries played a vital part, not only in Welsh, but in British history. It seemed, therefore, not inappropriate to follow the story of this natural unit in a single volume, tracing the changing interactions of Earth, Man and Time. There is a vast and scholarly literature on which to draw and I have put my sickle into other men's corn with deep gratitude, to trace the outlines of this story from earliest times to the present day. In common with other volumes in this series, the aim is to stimulate the reader to delve further into a rich storehouse whether in the library or the wide countryside of Gwynedd itself or, preferably, both.

In addition to the many distinguished studies on which this short account is based, I have become indebted to many friends, colleagues, public bodies, and companies for information, especially for 20th-century material. Professor E. G. Bowen and Miss Megan Ellis have read and advised on the work as it has advanced, and have offered valuable suggestions which have been gratefully followed. I acknowledge too the help of Mr and Mrs Glyn Evans, the Rev. Brian J. Mifflin, Mrs Freda M. Pearson and Mr J. Penrice who have read portions in which they had special interest. Miss Elisabeth Beazley and Dr Peter Ellis Jones have, with Professor Bowen, generously allowed me to base three of the maps on their own published work. Mrs Grace Corbett has drawn almost all the marginal illustrations. Mr James Hogan undertook the draughtsmanship and himself designed the Llandudno map. Mr and Mrs R. J. Rawcliffe converted my colour transparencies to monochrome; Mr M. L. Taylor has undertaken other photographic conversions, and Mr J. Penrice contributed drawings.

I have called on the resources of the National Library of Wales and, as always, had unstinted support and the generous help of the Librarian, Dr R. Geraint Gruffydd, and Mr Donald Moore and his Assistant Keepers in the Department of Prints, Drawings and Maps. Access to official statistics and other information has been afforded by several departments of Gwynedd County Council, the Manpower Services Commission (Gwynedd), Mr A. Finn, Divisional Officer for the Crewe Division of the Ministry of A.F.F., the Forestry Commission,

9

the Welsh Office, the Wales Tourist Board, Ynys Môn Borough and Arfon District Council officers, the National Quarrying Museum (Llanberis), the National Railway Museum (York), the Penrhyn Estate, Penrhyn Quarries Ltd., Anglesey Aluminium Metal Co., the C.E.G.B., Shell U.K. (Stanlow Refinery), and Crewe County Library and Colwyn Bay (Clwyd) Library whose staffs have tirelessly responded to my requests for published works. These and other indebtedness recorded in the acknowledgements have resulted in renewing or establishing many personal contacts of the greatest friendliness and my warm thanks are extended to them all.

March, 1983

•

Acknowledgements

I acknowledge with sincere gratitude the following additional sources for permission to use published and other copyright material: Map 1, the Welsh Office; Pl. 53, by courtesy of the National Railway Museum, York; Pl. 61, the Forestry Commission; Pls. 24 and 26, the Forestry Commission (and the kind agreement of the beneficiaries of the late Charles F. Tunnicliffe); Pl. 17, the Central Office of Information; all of which are Crown Copyright. Pl. 42, the Lady Janet Douglas Pennant and the National Trust Photographic Library; Pls. 1 to 5 inclusive, Snowdonia National Park Authority, Pls. 12, 13, 16, 18, 20, 25, 43, 49, 50, 59 and 60, the National Library of Wales together with permission to include a drawing of Sir John Owen of Clenennau. This last was featured in the *Atlas of Caernarvonshire* edited by Dr. Bryn L. Davies whose agreement was readily given. Pl. 11, supplied by the National Museum of Wales, who gave permission for drawings of Roman finds at Segontium to be included. Pls. 9, 40, 41 and 45, the Gwynedd Archives, and Mr. Bryn R. Parry together with Mr. Geraint Bowen, editor of *Atlas Meirionydd* who gave permission to include drawings of items in that Atlas, and Mr. Parry for a drawing of a Cambrian Railway bus; Pls. 63, 64 and 65 were provided by the C.E.G.B. (NW Region); Pl. 8 from the Cambridge University Collection (copyright reserved); Pl. 28, Shell U.K. Oil (Stanlow Refinery); Pl. 62, Anglesey Aluminium Metal Co.; Pls. 47 and 48, Messrs. Bamforth and Co. Ltd.; Pl. 56, Messrs. M. E. M. Lloyd and C. C. Green; Map 15, by permission of Mr. D. Lloyd Hughes, the map re-drawn by Mr. F. W. Jones and published in *Holyhead: The Story of a Port* by D. Lloyd Hughes and Dorothy M. Williams. For permission to copy drawings of prehistoric finds published in Miss Frances Lynch's *Prehistoric Anglesey*, the agreement of Miss Lynch and the Publication Committee of the Anglesey Antiquarian Society and Field Club. Drawings of the statues of Llewelyn the Last and Owain Glyn Dŵr are included by courtesy of the Chairman of Cardiff City Council; Bangor Cathedral from material supplied by the Very Rev. J. Ivor Rees, Bishop of Bangor and with his permission; old ploughs by kind permission of Mr. Hugh Davies and Mrs. Margaret Humphreys; medieval figures by permission of Messrs. D. Lewis & Sons Ltd. (the Gomer Press). Transport drawings by Mr. J. Penrice are by courtesy of the following: TSMV St Sillio, Mr. T. Stephenson; 'Myrddyn Emrys', the Festiniog Railway Co.; Cambrian Line loco., Oxford Publishing Co.; deck of the 'Scotia', British Rail; 'Tal y llyn', the Hamlyn Group; Irish Mail, Mr. E. N. Kneale; Llandudno tramcar, Mr. R. F. Mack; Orion bus, Gwynedd Archives; 'Snowdon', Prescott-Pickup & Co.; 'Cegin' and 'Blanche', Mr. P. J. Lynch; and 'de Winton', Mr. G. D. King.

I The Theatre of Gwynedd

Gwynedd's magnificent landscapes of mountains and coasts, lakes and valleys, have a natural beauty which is excelled nowhere in Britain. Its towering peaks dominate a scene which delights by its variety against a perpetual backcloth of massive ranges. Y Wyddfa's summit reaches 3,500 feet in height; four other peaks exceed 3,000 feet; and more than half the area of Caernarvonshire and Merioneth is above 1,000 feet, the average tree line. From Anglesey one can see the whole wide panorama of the Snowdon ranges in proud array, and in constantly changing light and weather. But in no part of Gwynedd are hills long out of view. The ancient strata, eroded, folded, invaded by igneous activity, are in places veined by metallic ores, and nearby rocks in two huge bands, metamorphosed by the heat from volcanic eras, have been changed into slate. Both ores and slate have played a significant part in the economic and human history of the harsh mountain environment. Only during the 20th century have dramatic new ways been introduced to revolutionise the economic possibilities within Gwynedd's heartland and they are now putting its barrenness to work.

Snowdon from the Cob, Porthmadog

The proscenium of this land is the Celtic Sea, its waters fringed by Scotland, northern England, and Ireland, as well as Wales. Sea girt to north and west, sea and ships have played a constant role in Gwynedd's story, bringing trade, and settlers, and new cultural elements during much of her history. So integral a part is the sea in Gwynedd's life, that for centuries it has linked her tradewise with Mediterranean lands and all Western Europe. It seemed, too, as if the mountains tipped the population coastwards, like beads across a tilted bowl, and the outlook has for centuries been westwards rather than eastwards, diverted and contained by the high spine of Wales' mountains. In the time of the Princes, eastward movement usually implied conquest, expansion, or resistance to invasion.

The Welsh were long a tribal people with a common system of law, a common social structure and language, even though everywhere there were lesser *pays* or human sub-regions crystallised out by Time. Bonds of enormous strength were forged, welded into political shape by their rulers from the Dark Ages onwards, and despite the re-shaping of administrative geography from the time of Edward I, an older regional consciousness has survived in many areas. In the time of the

Beddgelert

11

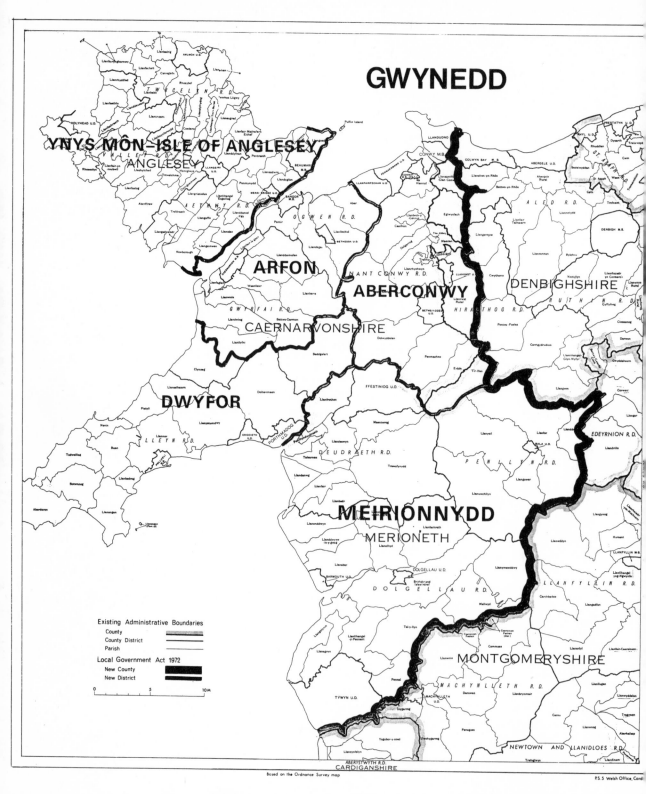

Map 1. Gwynedd: Administrative Divisions before and after April, 1974.

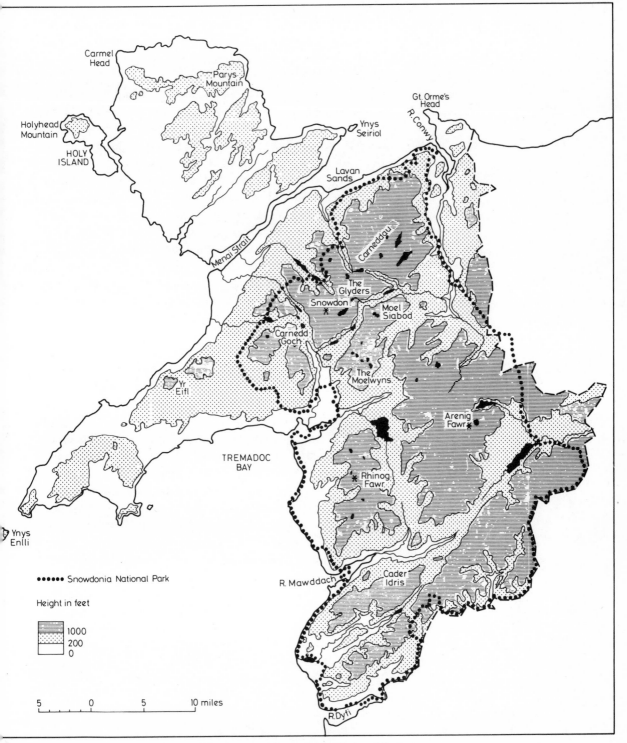

Carmel
Head

Parys
Mountain

Gt. Orme's
Head

R. Conwy

Holyhead
Mountain

Ynys
Seiriol

HOLY
ISLAND

Lavan
Sands

Menai Strait

Carneddau

The Glyders

Snowdon

Moel
Siabod

Carnedd
Goch

Yr
Eifl

The
Moelwyns

Arenig
Fawr

TREMADOC
BAY

Rhinog
Fawr.

Ynys
Enlli

•••••• Snowdonia National Park

Height in feet

	1000
	200
	0

R. Mawddach

Cader
Idris

5   0   5   10 miles

R. Dyfi

Map 2. Physical features and Snowdonia National Park.

Road to Lake Bala

Glen near Betws y Coed

two Llywelyns, Gwynedd reached the highest point of its sense of national identity, and became the spearhead of a move towards national unity. That it failed was the work of a tragic genius that from time to time has haunted Gwynedd.

But far from being the end of the story, Gwynedd's later history was to put many another play on her broad and lovely stage. Many were indeed dramatic. Many were of national importance, some re-shaping the course of British history as happened when the Tudors of Anglesey ascended the throne and brought to an end the Wars of the Roses. In the following century, Henry VIII, the second of the Tudor monarchs, achieved the Union of England and Wales. Since then, the stage has remained basically the same, but a long succession of new sets have contributed to the emergence of modern Wales. These 'sets' are the theme of the second part of this study, selected as highlights among the many other facets of the continuing story.

Though much has changed, much has remained: the natural scene, the climate, and many characteristics of the players, even though new actors have been added to the company, for to cross the lower Conwy or the Menai Straits is still to pass into *Pura Wallia*. One criterion generally applied, though it must not be pressed too far, is that of language. The four Welsh counties with the highest proportion of Welsh speakers are those from Cardiganshire to Anglesey. Gwynedd has three of them, and despite the progressive erosion of Welsh speech from the east westwards, the conformation and relative isolation of Gwynedd have operated to preserve it. Not surprisingly, mountainous Merioneth has a high proportion of Welsh speakers, though the percentage declined from 88 in 1901 to 72 in 1961 and to 70 per cent. in 1971. Caernar-vonshire in 1961 had 68 per cent., and there are still monolingual Welsh speakers in some of the more remote parts, for example, of the Llŷn Peninsula. Across the Straits, Anglesey's insularity is reflected in its 1961 figure of 75 per cent., the highest average for the three counties. Some of the more isolated villages in the interior of both Anglesey and Merioneth claim 90 per cent. and over. In Llandudno, where English influence is most evident, Welsh speakers become fewer, and when this is so access to the rich heritage of Welsh literature and legend in the original is lost. Yet the stage remains. Economy and people have the same physical background, and since the importance of conservation has been recognized, this landscape with its wealth of historic and cultural sites and its great beauty, is cared for, preserved, and treasured as never before.

14

II Before the Celts

MAN: a falling spark in the night of Time,
Life pulsing on dead planets,
A soul stirring at animal thresholds,
Illumed faith at the mind's twilight,
God-conceived and gods conceiving.

The oldest remains found in Wales are those of the so-called 'Red Lady' of Paviland in the Gower Peninsula in South Wales. Nevertheless, Man is of sufficient antiquity in North Wales to have experienced wide changes of climate and land conditions associated with the closing phases of the last Ice Age. The time-scale covering the changes which affected early Man so profoundly has been extended as a result of Carbon 14 dating, and it is now estimated that the first known inhabitants of North Wales lived in the last inter-glacial interval some 20,000 or more years ago. Their culture was Mousterian, a phase of the Palaeolithic or Old Stone Age, and the remains consist of several molars considered to be of Neanderthal type, together with the bones of rhino, hippo, and elephant—adequate proof of hunters with an ample food supply, and found in a cave at Pontnewydd in the Clwyd valley. Most of them are thought to have moved south to warmer climes when the next, and the last, great glacial advance (the Würm) made life difficult, yet some discoveries in a nearby cave at Caegwyn prove that a few at least remained in the area. In that cave were found tools of the following cultural period, the Aurignacian or Cresswellian as it is called in Britain, together with bones of woolly rhinoceros, cave bear, elk, wolf, and cave hyena, all indicative of extremely cold climatic conditions. More recently, proto-Aurignacian (Gravettian type) tools have been found in a cave on the Little Orme: so far the oldest known in Gwynedd. This culture was associated with the retreat phase of the last ice sheets, and it continued until it was superseded by the Middle Stone Age or Mesolithic cultures. By that time the excessive cold was giving place to a Boreal or sub-Arctic phase, and it gradually ameliorated still further, the glaciers shrank, and the ice retreated northwards.

The people of this remote age were additionally affected by slow upward and downward movement in sea level, hence in the extent of land surfaces and altering shorelines. Along Cardigan Bay during one post-glacial phase, land stretched far beyond the present coastline, and

A looped palstave,
Bronze Age

15

Early Times to the End of the Roman Occupation

Estimated Dating B.C.	Culture	Periods	Major Characteristics	Climate and land conditions
20,000	Old Stone Age (Palaeolithic)	Middle Mousterian. Upper Aurignacian	Crude stone implements. Hunters	Ice Age with Interglacial periods
8–6000	Middle Stone Age (Mesolithic)		Gatherers, fisher-men, hunters. Finer stone implements.	Boreal. sub-Arctic. Land elevated
5–4000	Neolithic		First farmers. Fine stone implements. Pottery weaving. Stone monu-ments	Atlantic. Land lower. Mild, wet climate
2000	Bronze Age	Early Beaker period	Beaker pottery. Great stone monuments	Sub-Boreal. Land re-elevated
1500		Middle. Native Develop-ment	Earliest metal workers	Cold, dry climate
1000		Late invasion	Hill forts. Fine implements	
500	Early Iron Age	A. Hallstatt and La Tène I. B. La Tène II.	Iron and bronze implements. Great hill forts	Sub Atlantic. Land lower. Mild and wet
A.D. 43+ to 390	Roman Occupation		Roads and fortresses. Native hill forts	Classical rainfall maximum

1. The Conwy valley above Betws-y-Coed.

2. Llynnau Mymbyr, Capel Curig and Snowdon.

3. Mawddach estuary.

4. The Cader range from the north-east.

5. Nant Dolgoch (lower fall).

6. The Holy Island coast near South Stack.

7. Presaddfed, Anglesey, prehistoric tomb.

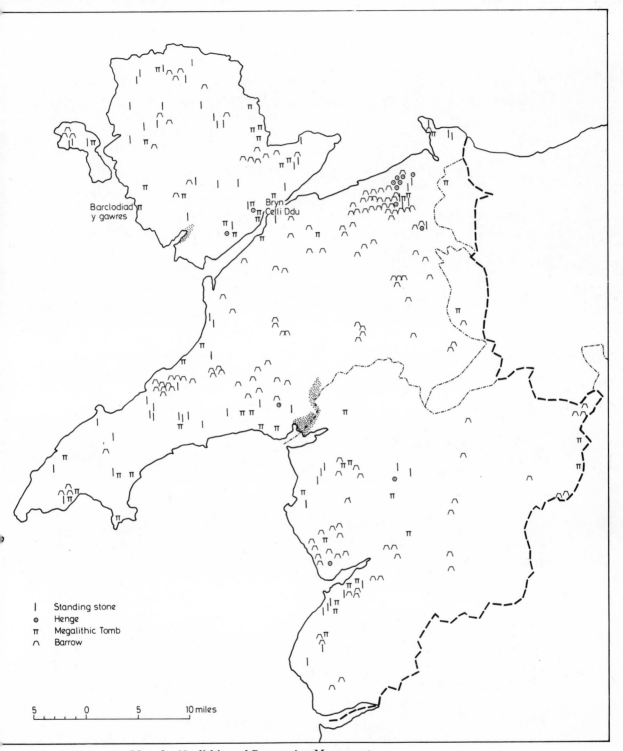

Barclodiad
y gawres

Bryn
Celli Ddu

| Standing stone
⊙ Henge
π Megalithic Tomb
∧ Barrow

5   0   5   10 miles

Map 3. Neolithic and Bronze Age Monuments

17

*Maen hir Llanfair
Ardudwy*

*Bronze Age axe head
(side view)*

the now-submerged plain off Merioneth and Cardiganshire is remembered in legend and folklore as the lost *cantref*—Cantref y Gwaelod. The petrified stumps of a once-living forest may still be seen at low spring tides off parts of these coasts. Conversely, after a period of submergence new caves and beaches were formed, and when elevation followed, they became the raised beaches traceable today around North Wales, their caves serving as shelter for early inhabitants. The pebbles of these beaches provided the stone for early crude implements such as scrapers and hammers. When the land was high relative to sea level, the Menai Straits were dry land, and Holy Island an extension of the main part of Anglesey.

The changing fauna and flora were of basic importance to the earliest human communities. Old Stone Age men were hunters and gatherers dependent on wild animals, birds, fish, shellfish, wild fruits, and nuts. But with the coming of the New Stone Age or Neolithic folk, farming first began in Britain, and soils became a significant factor in the siting of settlements. In a mountainous landscape these vary greatly from the bare almost soil-less slopes of the high mountains to the deeper, richer soils of the vales and coastlands, deposited by glaciers and rivers. These now became doubly precious for the crops and pasture on which Neolithic men depended to an increasing degree, and boulder clay, loams, sands, and alluvium became the sites of their cropland.

The earliest 'tools' of the Old Stone Age folk were pebbles and rock fragments either unaltered or so slightly chipped as to make their identification as tools uncertain. But the Gravettian phase displayed some refinement, and by Mesolithic times improving techniques had resulted in grading tools down to fine points and burins designed for hafting into wood, bone, or antler for spearing or throwing. The date now advances to about 8000 B.C. Little is known about the appearance of these Mesolithic folk, but, like the Aurignacians, they were definitely *Homo Sapiens,* and perhaps first appeared in Gwynedd about 6000 B.C. Hunters, gatherers, and strandloopers, they lived in a still harsh world, though with an increasing number of small animals, birds, and fish, from which to wrest a living, they became expert trappers, wildfowlers, and fishermen. Their tools have been found on open sites, the caves deserted, and they may well have graduated to the 'tame game' stage paralleled by the life-style of the Eskimos of northern Canada. Because so many of the Mesolithic sites are on open shores such as the Newborough Warren in Anglesey, where their implements can be picked up from the surface or from the dune sands, stratigraphical dating is difficult.

Early in the Mesolithic period pine and birch were dominant with more species gradually appearing, and berries and wild fruit, and nuts

18

for the picking. The land was still high compared with the succeeding Neolithic period, and many Mesolithic shore sites may therefore lie now below the sea. In addition to the coasts, these folk favoured river banks and lakeside locations, finding shelter probably under such cover as they could erect using branches and skins. The low-lying lands of Anglesey and Llŷn and the coastal edge of Merioneth attracted them, and their tools have been found at Newborough, Penmon, Porth Forllwyd (near Lligwy Bay), Trwyn Du, Aberffraw, and Llanbabo in Anglesey, those at Trwyn excavated from a Bronze Age cairn. In Caernarvonshire there are Mesolithic tool sites at Aberdaron, on Bardsey Island, on the Great Orme, and at Llanengan.

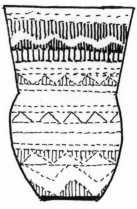

Typical Beaker

Soon after 5000 B.C. the New Stone Age dawned in Britain, and by the mid-fourth millennium, a Neolithic settlement is known to have existed at Llandegai, near Bangor, and at Capel Eithin (Gaerwen, Ang.). At both of these sites excavations have revealed a complete occupation succession from Neolithic to Romano-British. At Capel Eithin there are inhumation burials which S. I. White, director of the excavations, assumes to be early Christian. The first wave of Neolithic settlers may have come from Wessex. Later movements into West Wales, Cornwall, and the east coasts of Ireland were of Mediterranean folk, sailing north along the Atlantic waters which wash the shores of Iberia and western France, ancestors of many of the short, dark-haired people in those areas today. Neolithic and Mesolithic families doubtless lived side by side, but in time the earlier culture would be absorbed by the more advanced. By that time, the land was lower, the climate changing to the mild, rainy Atlantic phase, with oak and beech woods increasing. Many new species of both plants and animals became established in Britain during this period, and woodland clothed the coastlands, the valleys, and the lower slopes of the hills ever more richly. Pollen analyses in the Rhinog area of Merioneth carried out by M. F. Walker and J. A. Taylor have revealed that alder and elm were declining there, that patches of woodland were being cleared, pasture extending, but with alternating spells when woodland regenerated. In other words, primitive farming groups lived there, and it was the introduction of cultivation and pastoral farming which was one of the main bases of what has so often been termed the 'Neolithic Revolution': basic because it necessitated a settled life; because it made possible the storage of grain for the winter months; because animals on these simple farms provided a constant supply source of meat, wool, leather, and horn, as well as milk. Although stone still afforded the chief material for their implements, there were wood, bone, horn, and gut as subsidiaries. Originating centuries earlier in the Ancient East, it was also associated with the crafts of weaving and pottery making, but in

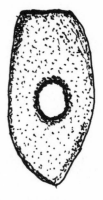

Early Bronze Age axe head

19

Megalithic tomb, Clynnog

Britain this New Stone Age lacked much of the sophistication of the cultures from which it was derived, and inevitably regional differentiation developed as is the case with all cultures that are transplanted.

The most impressive use to which the local geological material was put dates from the third millennium B.C., linking the late Neolithic and the Bronze Age through the building of the great stone monuments in a Megalithic Age. The splendid palaces and temples of the Orient associated with a similar stage of culture were undreamt of in North Wales, but their megaliths have never ceased to fascinate later peoples, and the questions they pose are far from being fully answered. Further, this is the first period from which visible evidences have been left in the landscape for all to see, that is, remains other than bones, implements, and other minutiae such as may be studied in museums, and Gwynedd is one of the parts of Britain best endowed with prehistoric monuments. They take the forms of standing stones, single or in pairs; stone circles (not very numerous); tombs or burial chambers; and so important are they that they seem to reflect an obsession with death and to imply a cult of the dead, for any or all of them may be associated with burials. More than that, we appear to have the first proof that the minds of men were working on problems other than the maintenance of life. In Neolithic times the tombs were covered by long barrows, in the Bronze Age by round ones, and not infrequently a stone circle enclosed them. Few, alas! have escaped the despoiler. Many may lie undiscovered. Recent research on the stone circles from north to south of western Europe has detected a remarkable uniformity between the angles and measurements on which they were designed. For example, there has been found to be a 'megalithic yard' of 2.72 feet, and the layouts indicate their use as astronomical 'clocks'. The selection, hewing, and transportation of these huge stones offer a further puzzle, added to by incisions such as spirals on the *meini hirion* (standing stones) and slabs inside the *cromlechau* (tombs).

Three recurrent types of *cromlech* have been distinguished. The earliest tend to be wedge-shaped or rectangular in ground plan, and to be late Neolithic or Beaker period (early Bronze Age), and those with distinct chambers are widespread all round the shores of the Irish Sea. Those of the Late Bronze Age fall into two categories, passage graves and portal dolmens. The portal dolmens have a tilted capstone and are found mainly in Llŷn and the Conwy valley, but both types have a passage leading to the inner chambers where were deposited the cremated remains of several individuals. The best known chambered tomb in Gwynedd is Bryn Celli Ddu in the parish of Llanddaniel Fab in south Anglesey. Originally within a stone circle, and the whole covered by a round barrow, this grave has been reconstructed, with

Capel Garmon tomb

20

the stone circle outside the mound. Visitors can walk through the massive stone passage into a broad chamber and gain a vivid impression of this type of monument.

Bryn Celli Ddu entrance

By this time the climate had changed to a colder Sub-Boreal dry type, and pastoralists could move their flocks to higher pastures in the hills. The population was now considerably increased so that although grain and flax were essential crops, the climates favoured pastoralism. About 2000 B.C. the invasion had occurred of Beaker folk, so named from the shape of their most characteristic pots, beakers used as cremation urns for their single burials. They brought with them the knowledge of metal, together with metal goods, but had no smiths. For the rest they were not unlike the Neolithic folk in their way of life. Known in the Orient from about 6000 B.C. metal working in copper, then bronze and gold, spread only slowly westward, but was general in Continental Europe by about 2000. It was brought as a craft to Britain about 1500 B.C. and the first British bronzes were moulded at that time. There appear to have been both founders and merchants, these last carrying their wares over a widening network of trackways over the hills and into the lowlands. It is their hoards, perhaps deposited for safety, which have provided us with a considerable wealth of Middle and Late Bronze Age weapons and ornaments. In addition there have been many chance finds. A flourishing school of metal workers was producing axes, spear heads, palstaves, razors, and jewellery between 1400 and 750 B.C. Hoards have been found at Menai Bridge, Ty Mawr (Holyhead), Beaumaris, Bangor, and Dolbenmaen, and these and many other finds leave no doubt about these people having had a strong warrior class. Irish gold also came into North Wales *via* Anglesey: very little in the Middle Bronze Age, but in increased bulk from the 8th century. A remarkable find was made at Gaerwen (Ang.) in 1856 of gold objects, including bracelets, ear-rings, and lock rings. Stone was still used for implements, but in addition to stone and bronze, jet and amber beads imply trade from Whitby and the Baltic.

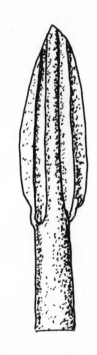

Bronze spearhead

The working of metals constituted another far-reaching revolution, and an increase in wealth as well as a degree of sophistication. Craftsmen and merchants added to the older farming elements, but there is no suggestion of increased domestic comfort, for the round hut still seems to have been predominant. The pattern of settlement, however, was controlled by the inexorable negative controls of a land in which the great mountain masses predominated.

21

III The Coming of the Celts

Simple hut circle

Perhaps the most significant event in Welsh history was the arrival of the Celts. Those who came to Wales were a Brythonic group, speaking a Brythonic or 'British' language. The Celts originated from an Oriental people who migrated into middle Europe and there from the 6th millennium B.C. passed through the Neolithic and Bronze stages of culture. By the 7th century B.C., influenced by the classical civilisations to the south and invigorated by their more northerly habitat and contacts, they had evolved a fully Celtic culture in the Hallstatt area (Austria), an early Iron Age culture noted for its elaborate chariot burials. They were farmers, craftsmen, and warriors, using both bronze and iron, evolving new techniques and new forms which were to flower, as never before, in a second, La Tène phase, much of their decorated metal work surpassing that of Greece and Rome. Equipped with horses they moved out in various directions: east into Asia Minor as the Galati; west into the Low Countries and across France as the Gauls, and finally into Britain as the Brythons and Goidels. Their language developed from Indo-European roots, and their dramatic sense blossomed into poetry and saga expressed orally. Their legends grew of the deeds of their tribal chieftains and the heroic age of our British Islands was born. Only in the 5th century of the Christian era did they become literate, but by then contact with four centuries of Romanisation, despite its thin veneer in the Highland Zone, was to produce surprising results.

The first wave of Celtic folk reached England about 500 B.C. and there introduced the Early Iron Age: a Hallstatt phase followed by La Tène I, known in British archaeology as the A type. A further invasion of Celts brought with them the more splendid La Tène II culture with its advanced design and art forms (Iron Age B), and yet a third group, the Belgae, mainly found in south-east England, the C type. The time of these various cultures affecting Wales is so far uncertain. Evidences of Iron Age A are slight except for the Llynfawr sword (Glam.) and the rather later bronze collar from Clynnog (Caerns.). Iron Age B extended into Wales, from south-west England possibly, and is associated with advanced forms of metal work and B Type hill forts. Some of the most important finds of British La Tène metalwork have been found in Gwynedd: the Harlech bronze mirror, the Trawsfynydd bronze tankard (both Merioneth), a 2nd-century bronze brooch

Composite hut circle

gold plated from Tre'r Ceiri (Caern.), and most magnificent and significant of all British Iron Age finds, the Llŷn Cerrig Bach hoard found when Valley aerodrome was being constructed in 1942–3 (Ang.).

It is probable that the first iron objects were brought by traders when Britain was still in the Bronze Age and that the full techniques were only slowly acquired by their smiths. Overlap, gradual acceptance, and slow change are characteristic of cultural transition. One of the outstanding features of the Celtic scene was the great hill fort, but it is now accepted that Late Bronze Age folk had already fortified many sites formerly thought to be solely Celtic, and that in some, refortification took place two or three times. The quality of their weapons and hill forts, even if comparatively simply defended by earthen ditches and palisading, testify to the raids and forays which must have taken place in the Bronze Age. But the Brythons were to prove far more ongoing, pressing their incursions into alien territory and settling. The tribal system strengthened under strong and doubtless ambitious chieftains, and the early Celts have been described by various writers as aggressive, ebullient, emotional, vocal, boastful, and artistic. They spread across Britain as far north as the Scottish Lowlands, and in its major regions different dialects developed, becoming distinctive branches stemming from Brythonic roots. In the Lowland Zone, in southern Scotland, and in Cornwall the language was eventually to be submerged and to disappear under the combined aggression of Anglo-Saxon, Latin, and Norman French, and to survive in its evolved form of Modern Welsh only in Wales. But by one of the curious contradictions of history, while few older forms of place-names survived in the Principality, many continued in use in England which, even with later modifications, have provided invaluable clues to the character of Primitive Welsh and even to the older British language.

The creative ability of the Celts was expressed in their craftsmanship, both utilitarian and artistic. They used bronze and iron, supplying an increasingly complex range of needs, including domestic equipment, weaponry, and personal ornaments. The introduction of the horse alone gave rise to previously unknown items being manufactured in metal, leather, and wood: wheeled vehicles, harness, horse bits, saddles, rings, reins, and yokes. Shields, swords, and daggers were made in either iron or bronze. Another minor revolution was brought by making iron ploughshares, and axes. Formerly land could only be cleared effectively by fire, but now trees could be felled and newly available land more quickly and easily tilled. During the La Tène II phase they developed styles based on those of the Greeks and Etruscans, their work eventually excelling the originals in metal decorative design.

During the first centuries both B.C. and A.D., a British-Gaulish cult,

Brooch design

Torc

23

*Bronze Age axe head,
Penrhyndeudraeth
(front view)*

that of the Druids, was practised in Anglesey. It was a pagan cult and its devotees gave the Romans a great deal of trouble, so much so that they are believed to have been exterminated in a Roman massacre in A.D. 47. Their importance to archaeology is the votive offering found in Llyn Cerrig Bach. This unique find consists of a wide variety of war gear, iron gang chains, bronze cauldrons, and, among other items, a sickle. But the most startling discovery was that the swords were made of fine quality steel; the most spectacular a magnificently decorated bronze shield, and the broken remains of a war chariot.

Early Iron Age settlements are the other notable feature of Celtic culture, doubly important because settlement evidence for earlier periods in Gwynedd is all too slim. Appreciable numbers of hut groups have been located, and of these the enclosed hut groups are the most interesting. Din Lligwy, near Lligwy Bay in east Anglesey, is thought to reflect Roman influence and to be a product of the Romano-British period. Enclosed within a stone wall, probably the residence of a chief or noble, the hut at the end opposite the entrance alone is circular, and slightly elevated. The other dwellings are all rectangular, and there is sufficient masonry remaining to make it especially easy to imagine the settlement as it must have been when it housed a living community.

Secondly, there are the hill forts, some small, some large, but all impressive, and more numerous in North Wales than in any other part of Britain except Cornwall. It is now accepted that many were Bronze Age in origin, taken over and elaborated by the Celts, and their defences strengthened. Some are believed to have been cattle kraals, these and others to have been used by the local inhabitants only in time of attack or threat of war, while yet others as in the case of Tre'r Ceiri at the high point of Yr Eifl (the Rivals) in north Caernarvonshire, where there were a hundred huts, were permanent settlements. Some are of the simpler A type, others the more complex B type. Defences therefore vary from the simple ditch and bank or the supplementation of naturally precipitous slopes, to those with deep ditches, walls, towers, and defended gateways. Univallate and multivallate, they come in varying shapes, sizes, and positions. Dinas Dinlle on the north coast of Llŷn and Caer y Twr on Holyhead Mountain occupy coastal promontories; Carn Pentyrch, Pen y Gaer, and Carn Fadryn (Caerns.) all inland; Tywyn y Parc, a low altitude promontory fort north of the Cefni estuary (Ang.). The B forts are usually multivallate, the A type defended by a simple bank and ditch, probably late 2nd century B.C., and only one of these survives in Merioneth.

So were laid the foundations of much of the region's later development and history, and not only in Wales, for the hill tradition is widely traceable in the hill villages and churches of southern Britain.

24

IV The Roman Impact on Gwynedd

The effective Roman conquest of Britain began when the Emperor Claudius landed in Kent in A.D. 43. The entire country was occupied by British tribes, and even the lowlands were brought only slowly under Roman control. Caratacus, the great champion of the British, only submitted in A.D. 51, and in A.D. 60 Queen Boudicca rose against Rome at the head of the Iceni. Hill peoples such as the Brigantes in the Pennines and the Ordovices of North-West Wales, fierce in their opposition, were far more difficult to subdue because of their skilful tactics in mountain warfare, and yet the control of Wales and the Pennines was essential if Rome was to control this new country of Britain. Further, each had valuable deposits of metallic ores as they were soon to discover: lead in Flintshire, south Shropshire, and the southern Pennines, gold in Dolaucothi, and the rich copper deposits of Parys Mountain and some lesser veins in the Great Orme. Eventually Wales was contained as a military zone together with northern England, but never urbanised apart from the south-east in what is now Gwent.

Auxiliary Roman soldier of c.A.D. 100

Climatically the Romano-British period experienced the later part of the sub-Atlantic phase. Dense woodlands of oak and birch clothed much of Gwynedd's surface, for the population was still sparse, and large areas remained virgin land. The old traders' tracks were of little use for a marching army, and the terrain offered innumerable problems for the movements of units of 500 or 1,000 men. From the base at *Deva* (Chester) roads were cut in due course across the relatively level stretches of the Flintshire and Denbighshire moorlands and the north-eastern flanks of the Snowdon Massif from Ro-wen to Aber, thence reached a crossing to Anglesey (though no roads were constructed in the island), and so to the important site of *Segontium*.

The Romans were skilled in both the planning and the construction of roads. They were not only the first to make metalled roads in this country, but provided a network so magnificently conceived that to this day it is followed by many major roads. The materials for building both the roads and the forts, which were sited at intervals of a day's march along them, were the first requirements. For the North Welsh roads they used Cheshire sandstone, local Welsh stone, and Welsh and Welsh Borderland lead. With characteristic speed and efficiency they summed up the geography of Wales and built a roughly rectangular 'box' of major highways, linking the four corners and

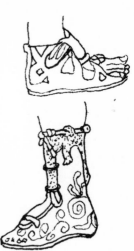

Roman shoes

25

Roman or British shield

excluding the peninsulas of Llŷn and Pembrokeshire. Within the box lesser link roads used the most practicable routes across country especially from east to west, and inland from major access points on the north and south coasts. The legionary fortresses of *Deva* (Chester) and *Isca* (Caerleon) were established at the north-eastern and south-eastern corners, and the lesser, but still important, forts at *Segontium* (Caernarvon) and *Maridunum* (Carmarthen) at the two western corners, and so the site of Caernarvon was selected and endowed with a regional importance in Gwynedd which was to re-echo throughout the centuries. Similarly, Chester's close relationship with the whole of North Wales was underlined by the link which this major route forged. It was the true gateway, sited near the fringe of the Flintshire plateau, where the lead of the Carboniferous Limestone beds was probably first extracted by the Romans from about A.D. 48. Recent excavations at Chester have revealed a pre-Flavian series of defences which must have been in existence for some years before being razed to make way for the stone buildings constructed from A.D. 68 onwards, and these dates may be assumed to be of significance in dating the making of the North Wales road.

Caratacus, the British chieftain, who marched west to support the Ordovices, was defeated in A.D. 51 at an undetermined site probably in the Borderland, and in the succeeding years up to the appointment of Suetonius Paulinus in A.D. 59, Wales was left in relative peace while the work of road building and the setting up of small forts went ahead. But for two years from A.D. 59, under the vigorous and ruthless policies of Paulinus, Gwynedd was penetrated, and the Menai Straits were crossed, probably at low tide or perhaps in flat-bottomed boats. Then with appalling cruelty this main centre of Druidism was attacked, and men and women alike put to the sword by troops of the Twentieth and some of the Fourteenth Legions. After that the Icenian revolt under Queen Boudicca required urgent reinforcements in East Anglia, and men were withdrawn from Gwynedd for the purpose.

Brick with 20th Legion stamp, Segontium

It was A.D. 78 before the Ordovices were finally conquered by Frontinus, but even after their supposed defeat, the Ordovices exterminated a Roman cavalry regiment. However, in that same year, Agricola, father-in-law of the historian, Tacitus, replaced Frontinus as governor. Anglesey was conquered, and the Ordovices were massacred with such appalling losses that it is more than probable that this led to the desertion of many of the native hut groups. G. C. Boon believes that there are strong arguments for dating the foundations of the timber fort at *Segontium* to that year. Anglesey was never to be under permanent Roman occupation, and as no Roman roads are known to

26

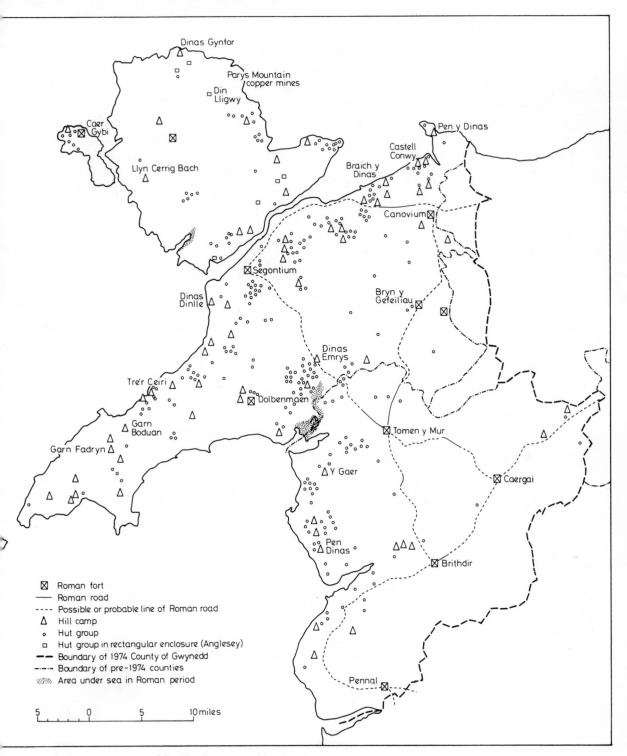

Legend:

☒ Roman fort
— Roman road
---- Possible or probable line of Roman road
△ Hill camp
○ Hut group
□ Hut group in rectangular enclosure (Anglesey)
▬ ▬ Boundary of 1974 County of Gwynedd
·—·—· Boundary of pre-1974 counties
░░░ Area under sea in Roman period

5   0   5   10 miles

Map 4. Roman and Native Gwynedd

Labels on map:
Dinas Gynfor, Parys Mountain copper mines, Din Lligwy, Caer Gybi, Llyn Cerrig Bach, Pen y Dinas, Castell Conwy, Braich y Dinas, Canovium, Segontium, Dinas Dinlle, Bryn y Gefeiliau, Dinas Emrys, Tre'r Ceiri, Dolbenmaen, Garn Boduan, Garn Fadryn, Y Gaer, Tomen y Mur, Caergai, Pen Dinas, Brithdir, Pennal

have been built in the island, access to the copper of Parys Mountain must have been by native trackways.

Thenceforth the Roman road linking *Deva* and *Segontium,* the only one in Gwynedd mentioned in the Antonine Itinerary, was of foremost strategic importance. It was the forerunner of others of which the routes varied in detail, but in some form or another 'the North Wales Coast Road' was to remain for ever a major artery. Serving the lead mines of Flintshire, it avoided both the worst gradients and the denser woodland wherever possible, reaching the Clwyd at *Varae,* the site of a small Roman fort somewhere near St Asaph (Llanelwy), and thence over the Denbighshire plateau to the crossing of the lower Conwy at Caerhun, where the fort of *Canovium* lies cheek by jowl with the small parish church on the farther bank of the river. Avoiding the difficult cliff-bound coastline west of the Conwy, the road made for the line of the old Bronze Age trackway from Ro-wen, dropping to the coast at Aber which it followed from there along to *Segontium.* From *Canovium* a link road connected the north with the west coast road by following the left bank of the Conwy to Bryngyfeiliau (Caer Llugwy) west of Betws y coed to the important camp which the Romans set up at Tomen y mur in western Merioneth. A second road also led from *Segontium* to Tomen y mur through the Quellyn valley, along the line of the present-day A 4805. The only other road in the Roman network within Gwynedd led (from Chester) to Bala and crossed southern Merioneth *via* the Wnion valley to the small fort of Caer gai, continuing westward to join the west coast road at Brithdir.

For over three hundred years *Segontium* was the most important Roman site in Gwynedd. At the angle of the north and west roads its specific purpose was the control of north-west Wales, with its hostile and warlike Ordovician population, and the tribes of Anglesey, to which a short crossing gave easy access at the western end of the Menai Straits, and opened up the way to the all-important Parys Mountain copper mines. Although *Segontium* was referred to in the *Mabinogi* and the *Historia Brittonum,* after the Dark Ages it seems largely to have faded from memory for centuries prior to the extension of Caernarvon up the hill towards Llanbeblig in the 19th and 20th centuries when the remains of the old fortress was used as a very handy 'quarry' for building stone. By that time not only the church, but the churchyard and vicarage had been built over a considerable part of the fortress, its history and significance alike forgotten.

But with the history of this as of other periods now being painstakingly re-written through the agency of the spade, three main excavations have so far contributed to re-drawing the plan of the major part of the site, and to the re-writing of some part of its

Legionary sword, Segontium

28

history. Moreover, the visitor can now follow the layout on the ground and see the permanent exhibition of finds, plans, and other exhibits in the Ministry of the Environment's museum built on the site in 1937. The first excavation was carried out in 1913 by members of the Cambrian Archaeological Association; the second by Mortimer Wheeler in 1921–3; and since 1925 when the site was bought and vested in the National Trust, excavation has continued under the auspices of the Ministry. Many corrections and extensions of the work have been carried out, including the discovery of the original defensive ditch near the north-east gate and a temple dedicated to the worship of the god Mithras, the only Roman temple within the Military Zone of Wales.

Gold 'crossbow' brooch, found near Segontium

Four periods have been distinguished in the history of *Segontium*. The strong probability is that it was founded in A.D. 78, a timber fort planned on a scale which suggests a garrison of 1,000 men, including infantry and part mounted. By the year 140, numbers as indicated by coins and other finds were probably less, but the fortress was then built in stone—Cheshire sandstone and tiles from Holt in the Dee Valley being used for a number of buildings, as well as local stone. Evidence of burning and damage to the aqueducts point to the possibility of an attack by the Ordovices; a second period of rebuilding restored the damage between 198 and 209, and saw the completion of the defences with a tower and a guardhouse. A bath-house was also constructed, but considerable gaps were now occurring in its occupation. Coins were fewer, and glass beads imply the presence of women folk also. In a fourth period after further damage about 369, the surrounding ditches were doubled, and bridges built across them to the gateways. Accommodation for the men was better, but the Romans were now facing trouble on three fronts. Irish Goidels were raiding and settling on the coasts of Wales and Lancashire. Picts were sweeping down on northern England, where the Romans no longer made any pretence of maintaining Hadrian's Wall, and, thirdly, the Saxons were raiding the south-east and east of England. A number of forts both in Wales and northern England were rebuilt as well as lookouts at sundry points along what was so soon to be called the Saxon Shore, but the end was heralded, and *Segontium* seems finally to have been degarrisoned in 383 apart from a handful of soldiers who remained until A.D. 390. A fortified Roman structure on the west bank of the river Seiont, where goods for *Segontium* were unloaded, indicates that the Irish sea rovers were a menace there, and the problem was probably considerably more serious at the port of Caergybi (Holyhead). Anglesey was outside the close jurisdiction of *Segontium,* but its valuable copper ores were probably exported by sea from the then tiny creek which lay below the present church of St Cybi (built within

Tinned bronze 'trumpet' brooch with late Celtic decoration (front and side views), Segontium

29

Roman lamp

Roman hot air flue

Altar to Minerva, Segontium

the Roman fort) near to where the inner harbour was constructed in the 19th century. The creek is now the site of Victoria Road. This early harbour had been used from prehistoric times, and the Roman fort was built to protect it. A wall of rock fell sheer to the creek, but above the cliff three other sides of a quadrangle, 250 feet by 150 feet, were walled, and a considerable portion of these Roman walls is still *in situ*. On the north-west corner was built a hollow half-round tower of a type fairly common on the Continent, but unknown in Britain except at Cardiff.

Merioneth, mountainous and lacking the regional significance of the more northerly parts of Gwynedd for the Romans, had a few fortlets along its roads. The most important was Tomen y mur, so named from the later castle mound or motte built inside the Roman enclosure. The walls and towers are in ruins and there is little to be seen, but its value lay in its function as a halt point on the west coast from *Segontium* to *Maridunum*.

By the latter half of the 4th century, the superb energy of Rome's initial thrust into Wales had indeed lost its original verve. Barbarian inroads into Europe threatened the very existence of the Empire, and in Britain, too, the Teutonic invaders could no longer be repelled. What then was the aftermath to be? Roman roads were sufficiently well constructed to serve native Gwynedd's needs for centuries to come, albeit in ill repair. But the fortresses fell into decay, and green Nature overgrew them until they were all but lost in memory. Even greater fortresses, including *Segontium*, have literally had to be 'unearthed' to trace their ancient plan. What then of any settlement which may have existed outside the crumbled walls? Recent excavations at *Maridunum* have uncovered a contemporary town adjacent to the Roman fortress. Now it is thought that similar revelations may at some time reward the spade in Caernarvon, where a settlement, perhaps of camp followers, may well have existed outside the walls and survived there for some time, or moved down to the site of the Roman harbour on the banks of the river Seiont.

The Romans departed, leaving undoubted bitterness and resentment behind in this area which had so long suffered suppression and even vicious punishment. But the Celtic West had gained far more from Rome than it realized in A.D. 400. Latin was to be spoken and written even during the Dark Ages. Concepts of law and administration had taken root. And now, as a result of the mounting information concerning early Christianity in Britain which has been traced during the past half-century, it is clear that it was thanks to the Roman army and merchants that it first spread here.

30

V Gwynedd in the Dark Ages

From the withdrawal of the Romans, Britain south of the Antonine Wall fell into a number of tribal territories under chieftains or war leaders, often self-styled princes. In the Civil Zone an aura of Romanisation tended to linger, and even in the Cambrian peninsula and southern Scotland there were traces such as the use of Latin personal names. More significantly, the seeds of Christianity were to take early root in the Highland Zone. The only unity in the 5th century was a common Celtic culture and by 800 this was to be overlain and hybridised by a Teutonic invasion which swept up to the borders of the uplands. One of the major themes of these 400 years is the struggle between the British and the Anglo-Saxons for supremacy.

Tracing the history of the period is fraught with difficulties, for written accounts are few, late, patchy, and far from reliable. Yet personalities and events emerge, the mists of prehistory disperse, and as the centuries pass up to the time of the Norman Conquest, an uncertain twilight spreads. In common with the rest of Britain in the 5th century, Wales had its tribal territories, each *gwlad* (territory or political unit) under a chieftain claiming semi-royal status, and many prepared to expand at the expense of their neighbours. There was a degree of social stratification. The 'nobility' held minor courts in their halls, had their own bards and poets, and were doubtless visited by peripatetic story-tellers, armourers, the makers of fine weapons, and jewellers. There were craftsmen and traders, though the British had no currency of their own in the post-Roman period, and are not known to have had any markets, trading being presumably by exchange and barter. Small groups of fighting men were attached to the leaders of the tribes, and during the 5th and 6th centuries monks, priests, and hermits became an addidional element in the population. Last came those who formed the greater number in the tribes: free tribesmen who were perhaps primarily pastoralists, and the bondsmen who lived apart from the free, and whose task seems to have been to produce the bulk of the crops and to plough and maintain the fields, not least to do any menial tasks which offered. In a mountainous region geography imposes very definite limits on the area suitable for tillage, and this is so also in Anglesey, in districts where soil is thin and rocks protrude, even in lowland. Where the land was sufficiently fertile, wheat and barley were raised, oats in the poorer parts, and flax and minor crops as they were needed. From the products of pastoralism and hunting, meat, milk and dairy produce, supplied a high proportion of the food, together with leather, furs, and wool. Leather had a wide variety of uses for clothing and household purposes. Very little pottery was made in the Dark Ages. Wood, turf, and stone supplied building material and fuel, but it is not known that any metallic ores were extracted unless on a minor scale, and smiths may have been more dependent on imports and on scrap. Houses, other than the halls of the nobles, appear to have been one-room crudely constructed huts, most of them round, but some rectangular or sub-rectangular.

Archaeology had little to offer concerning Dark Age settlement in Wales prior to 1950, but the last three decades have seen excavations of importance at Dinas Powis (Glam.), Dinas Emrys, Garn Boduan, and Castell Degannwy (Gwynedd), and Dinorben (Clwyd), all fortified hill sites, and at Pant-y-saer (Ang.). Dr. H. N. Savory, responsible for the work done at Dinas Emrys, traced five occupation periods extending through the Iron Age to the end of the 1st century A.D., through the Roman occupation's later years, and in the Dark Ages to the time of the Princes, but the Dark Age settlement being the most important. It was then a chieftain's dwelling described by Llywarch ap Llywelin, a 12th-century poet, as 'many ramparted', and the last defences built were those of the Dark Ages, the inner walls then or later. Legends innumerable adhere to this hill fort near Beddgelert, which overlooks one of the most important routes across Caernarvonshire. Welsh lore links it with Ambrosius Aurelianus, Arthur, Vortigern, and Caradoc, yet none is capable of proof. Castell Degannwy, excavated by Leslie Alcock in the 1960s, the site of the medieval castle on the east side of the Conwy estuary, was found to have a Dark Age fortification previously unrecognized and dating back to the 5th century A.D., but, unlike the medieval castle, it occupied only one of the rocky hillocks. It was traditionally a seat of Maelgwn, an early 6th-century king of Gwynedd, and it is of particular interest that it must have been as vital then as in the Middle Ages to hold the right bank of the river at this point, even though the river was the accepted boundary of this territory.

No great wealth of artefacts has been discovered in the Dark Age forts in Gwynedd. The pottery is in general crude and scanty, apart from some imported pieces, but a silver penannular brooch was found at Pant-y-Saer near Benllech, and a Chi-Rho monogram was on an imported sherd at Dinas Emrys, where there was also an iron smelting pit of the 4th or 5th century. During an earlier excavation at Dinas Emrys gold-plated bronze studs and a bronze bar with gold plating were found there, given at the time to a local landowner, but, unfortunately, they cannot now be traced. One very important result of the

'Pibgorn'—Welsh form of hornpipe

32

8. Aerial view of Tre'r Ceiri, a defended native hill town (*oppidum* type) of the Romano-British period. On a summit of Yr Eifl ('The Rivals') in north Llŷn, it is the largest Iron Age hill fort in Gwynedd. The village due east is Llanelhaiarn.

9. Dinas Emrys: an early engraving.

10. Din Lligwy, Anglesey, a Romano-British village.

11. *Segontium*, a reconstruction of the fortress and its setting.

12. Portion of the *Mabinogion* from the Red Book of Hergest (*Llyfr Coch Hergest*, 1375-1425).

13. Conway Bridge and Castle, a print by G. Pickering made between 1826 when Telford's Bridge was completed and 1848 when the first train crossed the railway bridge.

14. Conway Castle: the interior seen from the east end.

Gwynedd excavations is that the pottery and metal imports give ample proof of wide trade links in the Dark Ages with Gaul and Mediterranean countries.

After the Roman occupation, during which the speech of the Celtic population was British (or Brythonic), linguistic change continued rapidly. By the 5th century it had become Late British, and by the mid-6th century was still the very ancient form known as Primitive Welsh, a change of special significance in relation to dating the early poets Taliesin and Aneirin, though probably neither was born in Wales. The poems were passed on in verbal form, and pre-date the earliest surviving manuscripts, but the beginnings of Welsh literacy constitute a revolution which cannot be over-estimated in cultural development. In addition to the histories, the centuries were yielding a rich heritage of legend and poetry, and it is perhaps this which gives the most revealing picture of the people and the times, especially in the collection of romances known as the *Mabinogion*. Although they were written down only in the Middle Ages, they were indubitably of Dark Age origin. Many of them embody some part of the Arthurian legend. They were altered by centuries of re-telling, and in turn by Norman-French influence, before ever being written down in two Welsh collections, *Llyfr Gwyn Rhydderch* (The White Book of Rhydderch) and *Llyfr Coch Hergest* (The Red Book of Hergest) in the last quarter of the 14th or the first quarter of the 15th century. Interlaced with fantasy and romance, Celtic and Gallic, they are, nevertheless, rich and priceless pictures of Welsh life and culture in this difficult and fascinating era. If literature is the key to the character of a people, then we should find here something of the poetry and the colour which, at least in theory, distinguishes the Celt from the Anglo-Saxon. The earliest of the *Mabinogi*, 'Culhwch and Olwen', untouched by French romantics, displays all the imagination, the marvels, grotesquesness, and impossibilities that delight children. Surely they mark equally the childhood of a people: of Celtic folk emerging from the Early Iron Age to become the Cymry.

Arthur—'the Matter of Britain'—is drawn always as the great heroic figure, the great war leader, king, emperor, Count of Britain—who can know which?—Arthur taking counsel with a host of leaders from kings and bishops to great captains and wise men from many lands. The legend was taken up later by writers in many centuries, in turn by Mallory, Tennyson, and by later novelists and historians. His very existence has been doubted; his deeds argued over and disputed. Only in the last 30 years have archaeologists taken up the challenge to convince the doubters that there was a historic Arthur.

And so to the shadowy, but often very convincing, figures who move across the stage of history in the four centuries following the departure

Welsh harp

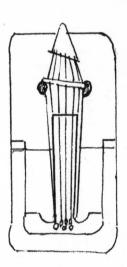

'Crwth'—a Welsh violin

33

of the Roman armies. Here is the heroic age in very truth. Here, too, are the tyrants, the traitors, and the villains. But the broad outlines of the rise of the Welsh dynasties, of the struggle to save Britain from the barbarians, and the eventual failure to stem the tide of Anglo-Saxon settlement across that part of Britain that was to become England can be sketched.

As hordes from Asia poured west into Europe, the threatened Roman Empire shortened its lines in self defence. Teutonic folk in turn—Angles, Saxons, and Jutes—began their westward thrust, and from the 360s were raiding the eastern and southern shores of Britain. With the virtual withdrawal of Roman protection from most of Wales in the 380s and the abandonment of the entire diocese of Britain before 410, a weakened country found itself under attack on all fronts. Irish were raiding the western peninsulas, Picts and Scots descending on the country south of Hadrian's Wall, and Teutons making landfalls on the coasts nearest to the Continental angle. A series of tyrannical 'emperors' seized power: Magnus Maximus (Maxen Wledig to the Welsh) slew the emperor Gratian in Gaul, and himself assumed power over Britain, Gaul, and Spain, until he in turn was overthrown by Theodosius. But his wife and sons and their descendants were closely associated with Gwynedd, particularly after his death. In the early 5th century Vortigern ruled Britain from Dyfed to Kent, and is credited with having invited Hengist and Horsa to the island to stem the inroads of Scots and Picts. But there is considerable uncertainty as to the events of this shadowy phase. The titles *Dux Britanniarum* (Duke of the Britains) and *Comes litoris Saxonici* (Count of the Saxon Shore) appear first to have been created in the late Roman period and to have lingered on through the 5th century.

At an unknown date in the 5th century there was sent to Gwynedd a British ruler, Cunedda, with his eight sons from his territory of Manau Gododdin, adjacent to the Firth of Forth. Their route is a matter of speculation, but it is of significance in that it may have been by the great land corridor which led across Shap and south to the Welsh Borderland (and Dumnonia) or by sea from south-west Scotland, routes of great importance in relation to British history in the Dark Ages. He is believed to have been the founder of a dynasty in Gwynedd and claims are made that the names of his sons are perpetuated in medieval local divisions in the area over which he ruled from Rhufoniog to Ceridigion. The reason for his migration is said to be that he was to help drive out the Irish (Goidelic) raiders and settlers from the western coastlands of Wales. Two other major figures appear, Ambrosius Aurelianus in the late 6th century and the great Arthur in the late 5th and early 6th centuries, both probably Romano-British, but major

Cross reputedly in Arthur's coffin, Glastonbury

antagonists of the Teutons whom they halted or delayed in their westward movement for many decades. That they failed to achieve permanent success in no way detracts from their heroic war. The battle of Mount Badon, reputedly Arthur's last but one (site uncertain), held up the advance of the West Saxons for some time. But the next battle, that of Camlann, was that at which he suffered his mortal wound.

The Cadfan stone in the churchyard of Llangadwaladr (Ang.) is a memorial to the king who ruled in Gwynedd in the 7th century when Wales was fighting a rearguard action against the English advance in the east. Wales and England alike were divided into political units or kingdoms, all contending for power and extension. Anglian Mercia had spread across to the eastern foothills of Wales; Anglian Northumberland dominated northern lands east of the Pennines, and under Ethelfrith its ambitions reached their peak. About the year 615 he led his forces across the Pennines, down through Lancashire and into Cheshire, where he routed the Mercians who were aided by the British at the battle of Chester, destroying the monastery of Bangor is y coed further up the Dee because their monks had prayed for victory against the Northumbrians. It was one of the many occasions when Gwynedd ranged itself with the Borderland counties to defend its own eastern flank. Gwynedd had underwritten an eastern frontier to and from which she advanced, and from which she was alternately repulsed for centuries to come.

Cadwaladr, renowned son of Cadwallon, succeeded his father. The royal seat is known to have been at Aberffraw, near Anglesey's west coast, but all attempts to trace the site of the *llys* have failed. Nearby is the village of Llangadwaladr which embodies his name. He reigned until 664, and, as the *Welsh Chronicle* has it, with his demise 'the crown of the Isle of Britain came to an end'. The failure of the British to stem the Anglo-Saxon tide was tragically implicit in the statement. Little is known of the years that followed, except that Cadwaladr was succeeded by princes who were not of the Cunedda line. Wales was now isolated, and the history of the next 100 years is confused. Mercia's star was in the ascendancy, and from 757 one of its greatest kings, Offa, marked *his* western frontier in 784 with the longest of all the Anglo-Saxon dykes. Extending from Northern Flintshire to the mouth of the Wye, its significance as a frontier line has doubtless been exaggerated, but its symbolic meaning was clear. Henceforth Wales was Wales, and England was the conquered realm to the east which had to learn from yet another people and their culture, while Wales though beaten back into the mountains was still free and British.

Typical prow of a Viking ship

VI Early Christianity in Gwynedd

Penmon Cross, Anglesey

As the 4th century drew to a close, there was little to indicate that the next 100 years would lead to a major crossroad in European history. Yet as Rome withdrew from Britain, the West stood on the very brink of changes which were to transform the entire character of society. These changes stemmed from two opposite forces. The early Barbarian migrations were already sounding the knell for the great Roman Empire, threatening the Roman and the Celtic world alike. But none then can have foreseen that the great darkness which they cast over western Europe would eventually be lifted by Christianity, at that time a comparatively little known, invisible force, which was to prove of unprecedented power. From the night of the Dark Ages, having routed the old pagan religions, Europe was to emerge with a culture and broad unity of beliefs which caused it to become known as Western Christendom.

The history of these remote centuries is still difficult to reconstruct as regards the extension of Christianity in Britain. It is slowly being built up from various sources and disciplines, and the last half century has witnessed considerable progress. During that time it has been approached from various angles: archaeology, linguistic studies, geographical and historical reinterpretations have all added something to the scant documentation. A further distinction must be made clear at the outset: that between the early growth of the Faith in the Lowland and the Highland Zones. To gain a balanced view of this complex subject of Christian origins in Wales it is essential to look first at a wider field.

Celtic cross design

The first indications of Christianity in Britain are tenuous. Tertullian in A.D. 200 spoke of the Gospel being preached in parts of Britain beyond Roman influence, and Origen wrote of it in 240 as a unifying force among the Britons, but both were far away from these islands. During the 3rd century, Christians were persecuted in many parts of the Empire, and it may have been so in Britain, but in the early 4th century the Emperor Constantine (306–37) was converted to the Faith. It must have been then or earlier than Alban, a soldier in the Roman army gave shelter to a priest fleeing from persecution somewhere in the vicinity of *Verulamium*. Alban was killed in reprisal, and the name St Albans commemorates his martyrdom. At some time during the 4th century Britain was nominated a Roman diocese, and it

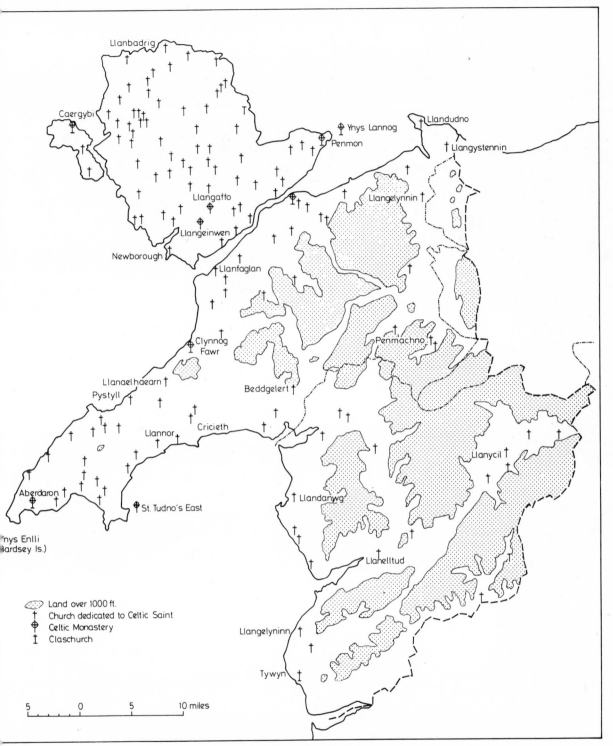

Map 5. Dedications to the Celtic Saints, after E. G. Bowen.

Llanbadrig

Caergybi

Ynys Lannog
Llandudno
Penmon
Llangystennin

Llangelynnin

Llangaffo

Llangeinwen

Newborough

Llanfaglan

Penmachno

Clynnog
Fawr

Llanaelhaearn
Pystyll
Beddgelert

Llannor
Cricieth
Llanycil

Aberdaron
St. Tudno's East
Llandanwg

Ynys Enlli
(Bardsey Is.)
Llanelltud

Land over 1000 ft.
Church dedicated to Celtic Saint
Celtic Monastery
Claschurch

Llangelyninn

Tywyn

5   0   5   10 miles

The Caelestis Stone in Llanaber church (5th-7th century)

is said that from that time Roman troops were ordered to inscribe the Chi-Rho sign on their shields. (Chi-Rho are the initial Greek capitals of Christ's name and are written X P.) Recent studies by a number of scholars including Charles Thomas and Kathleen Hughes have led to the contention that the history of early Christianity in Wales reflected Roman and Gaulish influences operating during, and for some time after, the Roman occupation of Britain. Later, echoes of Near Eastern and North African developments reached Wales by the Western seaways and became a powerful formative factor in Celtic Christianity. The Church in West Wales from the 6th century onwards was to proceed along very different paths from that in England as these two different trends merged.

It is now widely accepted that the seeds of early Christianity in Britain were sown by the Roman army and by merchants. In 314, British bishops attended the Council of Arles, and in 359 also there were British bishops at the Council of Rimini. In Lowland Britain some early Christian centres dating from the Roman period are traceable through place-names, some from archaeological discoveries. Kenneth Cameron has identified some 20 examples of widely-scattered places of which the names incorporate the element *eccles* (Latin *eclesia*, Prim. Welsh *egles*), meaning a church. Over half of them are in Lancashire, Yorkshire and the Welsh Borderland. Other evidences of the greatest interest have been turned up by the archaeologists from Carlisle to the south coast. They include mosaic floors and stones with Christian anagrams and the Chi-Rho sign. In Wales, pointers from the Roman period are less numerous, but the probability that Macsen Wledig's widow, Helena (Elen Luyddog), and their sons, who returned to Wales after Macsen's death, aided the extension of Christianity, is supported by the dedication of the church of Llanbeblig to her son Peblig (Publicus), which is on the actual site of *Segontium*; and that of another church to her son, Constantine, at Llangystennin in the Creuddyn Peninsula. Legend has it that Elen herself was regarded as a saint. There are a number of places called Llanelen in Wales and, more relevant to the present interest, a Capel Elen formerly existed in Anglesey, and Sarn Elen is a well-known road through Merioneth. There is a tradition also that many of the Celtic saints were of Mascen Wledig's family, though it is probably more correct to call it a cult, for the blood link is in many cases doubtful.

After the withdrawal of Rome the Church in Britain seems to have passed through a period of indigenous development, strengthened by contact with Gaul, and especially with Brittany, in a period when the western seaways again took precedence of land routes between the western peninsulas of Britain and France. However, the theory of

Early Celtic bell

38

mass migration between Brittany and South Wales formulated by Nora K. Chadwick is thought by some historians and geographers to need modification in favour of more limited movements and normal interchange between the two areas. During the late 4th century, the prelate and missionary saint, Martin of Tours, was exercising a marked influence on Christian thought and practice in France and in Gaulish Christian centres around Lyon and Vienne. They extended to Wales in what must be termed a Gallo-Roman phase in the Church's history. Bishops were appointed in Britain, but unlike those on the Continent, Welsh bishops served tribal areas, for behind the whole development of Christianity in Wales during this period must be envisaged not an urban society with a comparatively sophisticated culture, but the rural and tribal ties and practices which for centuries more were to characterise Welsh society.

White Monk of Cymer Abbey

The second phase in the history of Christianity in Wales has recently been developed by E. G. Bowen in an address given on the occasion of the 800th anniversary of the building of St David's cathedral. During the lifetime of St David in the 6th century, Pelagianism was among the influences which were filtering into Wales both from Ireland, where Pelagius, an Irishman, originated, and through Gaul where the heresy was rife. In the critical 6th century, St David (Dewi Sant) raised a strong voice to exterminate it, and in turn was deeply affected by the type of monasticism being practised in eastern Mediterranean lands. Christians were being persecuted in the Roman provinces of Western Asia and Northern Africa during the 6th century, and, as a result, many fled into the deserts to live as hermits. Their cult of extreme asceticism was reflected in time in Gaulish monasteries. The practice of simplicity and poverty in his monastery spread and found favour throughout Wales. So, too, did the eremitic cult of the desert fathers, some of whom, having fled from persecution, set up monasteries in the deserts of North Africa and the Near East, while others became solitary hermits. The 'Church' in Wales was set even more firmly on a course of resistance to the authority of Rome, and some of the great medieval Celtic monasteries were founded at this time.

The unresolved problems of the early history of the diocese of Bangor may well be linked with this period and its controversies. Like St David's, its cathedral also is set in a valley near the coast invisible from the Straits. At that time the importance of the western sea routes to Wales, as distinct from the land routes to Lowland Britain, was further enhanced by the growing menace of the Anglo-Saxon attacks and their advancing settlement front in the eastern and southern coastlands of the Great Plain. As the Dark Ages overtook the Britons of these Lowlands, churches and monasteries were ravaged and the

Bangor Cathedral

39

HIC IACET *gravestone, 5th-6th century, Penmachno*

light of Christianity was dimmed. The Celtic 'Church' in the West, however, was enabled to go its own way. That way reflected the diverse influences of earlier centuries, and was clearly set on a course which resented Rome. There is no ancient dedication to St David in North Wales, but his influence was nevertheless widespread, and the early 'Church' in Wales from the 6th century onwards diverged in many respects from that in England. The evidence of its extension is widely visible over the landscape in every part of the country, nor it is yet determined how far beyond the boundaries of Wales proper it may be traceable. Churches with dedications dating from these early centuries (though the fabric in almost every case is no longer original), are to be found nearly everywhere, while others of which the dedications were replaced on later Normanisation are memorialised in place-names.

Archaeology has added further knowledge of the early period. In 1950, the late V. E. Nash-Williams published his major study of the Early Christian Monuments, and his Group I included epigraphical monuments of the 5th and 6th centuries. They are in most instances rough memorial slabs, but formulae which were engraved on them indicate the Christian character of the burial, for instance, HIC IACIT (Here lies), IN HOC TUMULO (in this tomb), incised low relief crosses, and the Chi-Rho monogram. They are most numerous in Wales, and especially in the western peninsulas and Anglesey, but they extend into Breconshire and Herefordshire, into mid-North Wales, and Cornwall. A second type in Group I are inscribed in Ogham, an early Irish alphabet, and some of these were also associated with Christian burial. The two distributions interlock. Many of the first type are traceable to Gaulish immigrants, and some are believed to be memorials to Christians who had fled from Roman Britain. Only three of these stones are datable with any accuracy. One is in Carmarthenshire, the other two in Gwynedd. At Penmachno, near Betws y Coed are two of these early slabs, and one of them in addition to having the Chi-Rho monogram is the earliest that it is possible to date with accuracy. As it states, it was erected IN TEMPORE IUSTINUS CONSULIS (in the time of Justinus the Consul) and the consular lists give this as the year 540. Roman capital inscriptions were succeeded in time by the more flowing uncials, and the earliest datable uncial inscription is also in Gwynedd set in the church wall at Llangadwaladr in Anglesey. It is a horizontal memorial slab to Cadfan which reads CATAMANUS REX SAPIENTISIMUS OPINATISIMUS OMNIUM REGUM (Cadfan king, wisest and most renowned of all kings). The church into which it is built was founded around 664 or 684, and the memorial is doubly important because it is the first on which the true cross can be dated.

The Celt is by nature deeply religious, and revivals have occurred

40

more than once in Welsh history. The Welsh responded with warmth in the 5th and 6th centuries to a major missionary undertaking. Celtic Christianity extended through the work of bishops, not with a territorial limitation, but with a roving commission, through heads of the Celtic monasteries, and last, but of very great interest and influence on society and the landscape, the wandering monks or *peregrini*. It was these last in particular who brought about the founding of the widely distributed small Celtic churches which are so characteristic of the Welsh scene. Some have fallen into ruins never to be replaced, but the majority were rebuilt as parish churches all over Wales from the early Middle Ages onwards, and many retain their early simplicity. Nor are they confined to the Principality as we know it today, but are numerous in south Herefordshire, and there are a number in the other Welsh Border counties. They were to reach their greatest density in Anglesey where there is a higher proportion of habitable land, and they are remarkably evenly distributed over the island. In the rest of Gwynedd they are situated at varying heights even up to and above 1,000 feet O.D. They occupy a variety of sites: islands such as Enlli (Bardsey), Ynys Seiriol (Priestholm or Puffin Island), and St Tudwal's East (all originally monastic); innumerable coastal sites such as Llandanwg old church and Morfa Dyffryn (Mer.); cliffs near to a landing place as in the case of St Tudno's on the Great Orme and St Cybi's within the Roman fort at Caergybi (Holyhead); sheltered valleys near the coast, for example Llanelltud (Mer.); or well inland as notably the series in the upper Dee valley on a presumed Roman road in east Merioneth; or high on a hillside as is Llangelynin (Caerns.).

St Beuno's church, Pistyll, on the Pilgrim Way to Bardsey Island

The recurrent *llan* element originally meant an enclosure and came to be associated so many times with the enclosure in which lay the church and the hermit's cell and his small patch of land, that it acquired the same significance in place-names as church has in English. The original church would be a simple building of turf, wood, or rough hewn stone covered with thatch, and the hermit's cell most likely a round hut similar to that of the families to which he ministered. It was usually the *peregrini*, the wandering 'saints' who founded the church, or a monk who wearied of community life. If he were so fortunate as to select a site where a spring supplied the essential water, or could dig a well, it became regarded as a holy well and was used as a baptistry. Some idea of the early complex can be seen at Penmon, and at Llangybi (Caerns.), though the buildings are doubtless much later in origin, as are the small rectangular sanctuaries so characteristic of the Welsh scene. For food, the 'saint' was in part dependent on the local community, and G. R. J. Jones has suggested that sites near a bond vill would be a natural choice. It is now generally agreed that the bond-

St Buan, Clynnog Fawr, church window

41

Holy Well, Penmon

men's vills arose in post-Roman times, but declined from the 12th century, leaving the church isolated, and giving today a false impression of a loneliness which was not original. Many of the Celtic saints moved from place to place on their mission, and Professor Bowen has traced the 'cult' areas of the saints whose names recur. In Gwynedd there are a number of these, the one most frequently remembered in dedications of churches, holy wells, etc., being that of St Beuno, a descendant of Powysian princes. In addition to holy wells and chapels, two churches are dedicated to him in Anglesey (Aberffraw and Trefdraeth), six in Caernarvonshire, all in the Llŷn Peninsula, and two in Merioneth (Gwyddelwern and Llanycil). Clynnog Fawr, originally a monastery and later a *clas* (collegiate or mother church) was to be the most important. His 'cult' also extends into eastern and mid-Wales and if his associate saints are added becomes very impressive indeed. St Deiniol is the dedicatory saint of the cathedral in Bangor, and of a parish church in the city as well as of Llanfor and Llanuwchllyn in Merioneth, but no other dedication occurs more than twice in Gwynedd churches.

It was an austere life for the *peregrini* and a remarkable series of journeys is associated with them. Where they picked suitable sites, later towns have arisen, and Bangor is the outstanding Gwynedd example, dominating its ecclesiastical life from early times, and disseminating learning when the darkness was greatest. But perhaps .the outstanding features of the early Christian missionary movement are its universality within Wales as well as in other Celtic countries, and the travels of both the laity and the priesthood in this epic period.

An 18th-century print of Bangor

VII   The Shaping of Gwynedd

The centuries from the isolation of Wales behind Offa's Dyke to the defeat and death of Llywelyn the Great in 1240 saw Gwynedd rise to become one of the most powerful and influential states within Wales. It was a period of considerable change in society, of notable achievements in the field of literature, especially poetry, but in the realm of politics events leapt to points of high drama. Rulers of the medieval *gwledydd* (states or territories), some of them great kings or princes, some tyrannical and grasping, and most of them land-seeking and power-hungry, were the actors who moved unendingly across the political scene. The country was an assemblage of commotes which were the territorial expression of tribal entities, age old and socially cohesive. But they were a warrior-based society also, and wars of ambition, wars arising from internecine quarrels, broke out with unhappy frequency when there were no longer external enemies readily available for a fight beyond the Dyke. Skilfully managed by their chiefs, these conflicts could lead to the coalescence of commotes into greater entities, and these in turn might be further enlarged through inheritance and marital ties. So arose three 'kingdoms' of major importance, their interests interlocked: Gwynedd in the north-west, Powys in the north-east, and Deheubarth in the south-west. But in the late 11th century, within a very few years of the Norman Conquest of England, the Welsh Borderland was embroiled with a new enemy as the Normans poured into eastern, and soon afterwards into southern, Wales. Only in North Wales were their efforts to be baulked as for 200 years victory and defeat see-sawed back and forth between Welsh and Normans.

The details of these 500 years are too long and too complex to be related in a volume of this length, so it must suffice to follow the patterns of the wars between the Welsh kingdoms, their expansion and recession, and the impact of Norman aggression on the country's internal history. The patterns are brilliantly clear: the underlying factors involved, and still in many cases obscure. Of the three major kingdoms, it was Powys with her long frontier in the east marked by Offa's Dyke, and her east-facing valleys offering easy access to the interior, which was the most vulnerable.

It was Powys and her smaller neighbours, Brycheiniog and Gwent to the south, which were the first to feel the harshness of the Norman

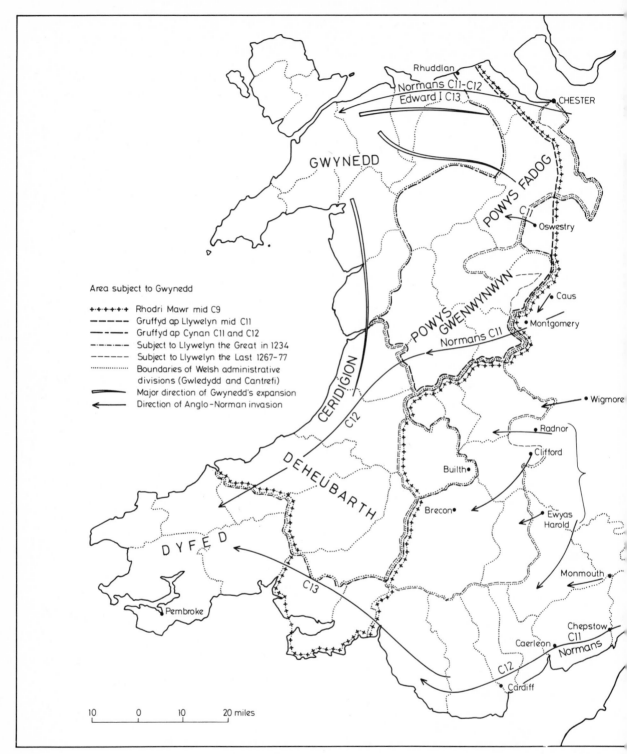

Map 6. Wales; Gwynedd's Expansion

Area subject to Gwynedd

+++++++ Rhodri Mawr mid C9
-------- Gruffyd ap Llywelyn mid C11
--·--·-- Gruffyd ap Cynan C11 and C12
-·--·--·- Subject to Llywelyn the Great in 1234
-------- Subject to Llywelyn the Last 1267-77
·········· Boundaries of Welsh administrative
            divisions (Gwledydd and Cantrefi)
══════ Major direction of Gwynedd's expansion
◄────── Direction of Anglo-Norman invasion

GWYNEDD

Rhuddlan
Normans C11-C12
Edward I C13
CHESTER

POWYS FADOG
C11
Oswestry

POWYS-GWENWYNWYN
Caus
Montgomery

Normans C11

CERIDIGION
C12

DEHEUBARTH

Wigmore
Radnor
Clifford
Builth
Brecon
Ewyas Harold
Monmouth

DYFED
C13

Pembroke

Chepstow C11
Caerleon
Normans
C12
Cardiff

10 0 10 20 miles

44

heel as the early castles and lordships were set up from Chester to Chepstow. Three border earldoms were created: Chester, allotted to Hugh d'Avranches; Shropshire, to Roger Montgomery; and Hereford to William Fitzosbern—each established with the prime purpose of promoting the conquest of Wales. Prior to this there had been internal wars for nearly three hundred years in a period when Wales had not begun to think of itself as a political entity, although the term *Cymry* (compatriots) was beginning to be used. The high proportion of mountainous land gives to the Cambrian peninsula a certain uniformity: it fails signally to offer unity as an easy gift, for the effect of its conformation is centrifugal. To its more able and distinguished rulers must be accorded the primary credit for contributing to the formation of the kingdoms, and later recognizing and fostering the possibility of nationhood. Gwynedd and Deheubarth raised the most outstanding of these men: Rhodri Mawr, founder of the dynasties of both Gwynedd and Deheubarth; Gruffydd ap Llywelyn, Owain Gwynedd, and the two Llywelyns, all of Gwynedd; and Hywel Dda and the Lord Rhys, both of Deheubarth. Each of these had a measure of greatness; each had strength of purpose; each achieved the territorial expansion of his realm; and Hywel Dda, the Lord Rhys, and the two Llywelyns had the wider ideal of some type of unity for the whole of Wales.

Dolbadarn Castle

External enemies were a recurrent menace during the reign of Rhodri Mawr. The first Viking raids on the wide open shores of Gwynedd took place in 850 or 851, coincident with the Danish efforts to oust the Norse from Dublin. Once again the emphasis was on the western seaways and many more such attacks were to take place in the next 200 years. During the late 9th century when Gwynedd was free from incursions by Irish Vikings, attacks from the east were resumed as Danes from York swept across northern England, captured Chester, and advanced into Gwynedd. Again during the 10th century there were periods of sea raids and towards its later years Anglesey was actually conquered. Coastal settlements were once again vulnerable. The *clas* church of Clynnog Fawr was damaged, and the monastery of Tywyn desecrated. B. G. Charles has suggested that the 2,000 prisoners they are said to have taken from Anglesey may have been sought as slaves. Yet the ease with which enemies may become allies was demonstrated when, in 1087, Gruffydd ap Cynan sailed with a Viking force which he had recruited in the Orkneys to support his claim to the throne of Gwynedd. After he acceded, tradition has it that he allowed many Norsemen to settle in his kingdom, but there is no evidence of this recognizable on the ground. Great Orme's Head, Priestholm, and the Skerries are scanty examples indeed of Scandinavian place-names in North Wales. There is more basis to the tradition that, although the

Irish continued to raid, they also made settlements in Gwynedd.

In common with the rest of Wales, she was to be embroiled in internal and external problems throughout this troubled period. She counted as her enemies at one time or another Norse, Danes, Mercians, and Normans, so that there were phases when she lay under threat from west, north and east. But the major themes of these centuries were strife between the Welsh kingdoms themselves and the determined pursuance by the Normans of their policy of conquest. Rhodri Mawr's wide realm in the 9th century embraced more of the country than that of any of his successors apart from Llywelyn the Last. It included all North Wales and Powys, but did not extend into Dyfed. At his death the Welsh laws of inheritance allowed this large unit to be divided between his three sons, and in 878 Gwynedd proper went to Anarawd from whom sprang the royal line of Gwynedd; Ceredigion to Cadell, though the extent of Cadell's portion is unknown and may have been wider; the share of Merfyn, his third son is uncertain. With boundaries being based on groups of commotes and the complexities of succession complicated by inheritance laws, intermarriage, conquest, and negotiation, the extent of the kingdoms may be seen as having been subject to all too frequent change. The heartland of Gwynedd lay west of the Conwy and north of the Dyfi, perhaps the nearest of all Welsh divisions to be a true *pays* and the only constant in centuries of shifting territorial combinations.

Dolwyddelan Castle

The internal geography of Wales operated as a constant theme in Welsh history in these four vital centuries. The movement of troops was wherever possible along the old Roman roads or through the major valleys and mountain passes. So movement in or out of Deheubarth was along the west coast Roman road and by valleys which led south-west, south, or south-east, but her northern flank was a difficult mountain mass. Powys had open valley routes that led eastward and northward, but was blocked to the west and south except across passes westwards which facilitated her expansion to the head of the Dyfi estuary. Lastly, Gwynedd was accessible by Roman ways south and east, her other outwards directions, especially to the south-east, more difficult. But the Welsh had one major tactical advantage against their opponents from the east in that their mountain guerrilla skills made it simple for them to retreat into the hill fastnesses where the enemy could not follow.

Deheubarth, and indeed Wales, had reason to be grateful to Hywel ap Cadell who succeeded to the whole of Dyfed in 920. Gifted and beneficent, he was to become the ruler of all South-West Wales and to occupy the throne of Deheubarth for about thirty years, going down in history as Hywel Dda (Hywel the Good). His contribution to posterity was the systemisation of the laws not only of his own realm but of the various Welsh *gwledydd*, including the Venedotian laws of Gwynedd. The value of his unification of many of the more important laws and his consequent contribution to law and order is incalculable.

Indeed, years of confusion and internal troubles followed in Deheubarth after the death of Hywel's grandson, Maredudd, in 999, but in 1039 Maredudd's grandson, Gruffydd ap Llywelyn, became the king of Gwynedd, reigning until 1063, the eve of the Norman conquest of England. He was a brilliant soldier, and his kingdom eventually embraced not only Powys but Deheubarth, so that Gwynedd extended over almost all Wales except for part of the south and south-east. The events which led up to this territorial extension are by no means known in detail. Most important is the fact that Gruffydd was a contemporary of Edward the Confessor, the weakness of Edward in sharp contrast with Gruffydd's strength. He was also ruthless. Sweeping into Mercia, he ravaged the Borderland, and turning west meted out the same treatment to Dyfed. In 1055 he concluded an alliance with Mercia, only to break it, capturing Hereford castle and looting the city and the new cathedral. The annexation of Gwent and Morgannwg followed, but in 1062 and in 1063 reprisals came *via* the North Wales coastal route, Harold invading Gwynedd *via* Chester to find that Gruffydd had taken avoiding action by sea. In the latter year, 1063, the year of Gruffydd's death, North Wales was ravaged by Harold and Tostig of Northumberland. But already the fifth column was at work in England. Harold was proclaimed king on the Confessor's death, but was killed himself at the decisive battle of Hastings. The Lowlands lay open to yet another conqueror. Parallels with the Norman strategy are not hard to find.

In 1081, there were civil risings in Gwynedd where Gruffydd ap Cynan was laying claim to the throne. Earl Hugh of Chester seized the moment and invaded. It was the first of many such Norman thrusts across North Wales. Robert of Rhuddlan was killed in the affray, and Gruffydd taken captive, lingering as a prisoner in Chester castle until his escape in 1087. Free at last, he set about marshalling his forces to reply to the Normans in kind, plundering Rhos and Rhufoniog as he went, he planned to advance on Chester. But Hugh met him and pressed through to Arfon and Anglesey, establishing a pattern of thrust and counter-thrust which was to be repeated many times before Hugh's death when, from 1101 to 1114, Gwynedd regained the overlordship of all North Wales. Before the latter year, Henry I was on the throne of England and led yet another attack with Alexander of Scotland as his ally, bringing Gruffydd to his knees, fining him, and forcing him to pay homage to himself as king.

Owain Gwynedd had succeeded his father in Gwynedd in 1137 and he took advantage of the situation in England, extending and consolidating his kingdom, still shattered after so many Norman successes. But with the accession of Henry II in 1154, the active process of Normanisation was resumed. In South Wales, the key castles of Carmarthen and Llandovery were already lost by the Welsh, and Norman manors and lordships covered the width of the country. The soft underbelly of Deheubarth's southern flank had been invaded to some purpose. But Rhys came to the throne of Deheubarth in the year following Henry II's accession, strong and determined, and he forced Henry to acknowledge him and to recognize the independence of his kingdom. Distant though it may seem to be from the affairs of Gwynedd, the stand taken by the Lord Rhys was important because Deheubarth was made into an invaluable buffer on its southern side, enabling Owain Gwynedd to concentrate on his eastern approaches.

Armourer

With a view to the conquest of Gwynedd itself, Hugh had followed his early success by establishing strongpoints at Degannwy, Bangor, Caernarvon, and at Aberlleiniog in south-east Anglesey, overlooking the Menai Strait. Such was his optimism in the 1080s, but these simple defences were to serve either side as the see-saw of advance and retreat continued along this major coast route. In due course, some fell into ruin, others were replaced by strong masonry castles.

The 12th century was one of constant troubles in Wales, and in 1165 when Deheubarth was experiencing widespread revolts, Rhys was aided by both Owain Gwynedd and Owain Cyfeiliog of Powys in a joint attempt to stem Henry II's further bids to subdue the independent Welsh. The two Owains moved into Dyffryn Clwyd and Henry set out to challenge them, but the Welsh mountains and Welsh weather combined to defeat him, floods stopping his army as they approached the Berwyns, so that he was forced to retreat. But for the Welsh forces, the Berwyns offered shelter to these Welshmen who were experts in guerrilla warfare, and from its high fastnesses they quietly watched their enemies retreat. By 1167, Owain Gwynedd had destroyed the castles of Rhuddlan and Basingwerk and was master of Tegeingl. Dying in 1170, a prince, not a king, he left Rhys as the most powerful figure in independent Wales. Of this Owain the *Welsh Chronicle* recorded that 'he was a man of great goodness and passing great nobility and prudence'. He and Rhys together had done much in a critical century to retard the Normanisation of Wales.

Gwynedd was in better case. When Llywelyn ap Iorwerth was born in 1174, two of his uncles ruled over the country: Rhodri to the west in Gwynedd uwch Conwy; and David to the east in Gwynedd is Conwy. At the age of 14, Llywelyn challenged both, and with the aid of two cousins he drove Rhodri from the kingdom, and in 1194 defeated

48

15. Beaumaris Castle: the moat and outer curtain wall.

16. Caernarvon Castle and Town, a print by G. Childs, *c*. 1845.

17. Castell y Bere, the excavated ruins of the most elaborate of the castles of the Welsh Princes. Abandoned by Edward I some time after Madog's rebellion.

18. The Great Seal of Owain Glyn Dŵr.

19. Tal y Llyn.

20. Harlech Castle: 1824 print. Note that the sea still came quite near to the foot of the hill.

21. Harlech Castle Gatehouse. The most massive and develope in any of Edward's Gwynedd castles, its total depth evident from this access tunnel.

David in battle. Firmly on his grandfather's throne, he set himself the task of gaining ascendancy over an increasing number of Welsh chieftains. By 1200 all North Wales was in the hands of this determined and assertive prince, and the times were changing. The 12th century had not been unaware of new concepts and methods in England. Intermarriage with royal and noble houses in England was not uncommon in the Marches and far from unknown in Wales, and Llywelyn was among the growing number prepared to accept the advantages of such new ideas as were filtering through a number of channels into Wales. The reasonableness of primogeniture was one such, the development of the economy another. He also weighed the advantages of swearing fealty to the English monarch, and in 1201 in return for so doing King John recognized Llywelyn's overlordship in his now extensive lands. Llywelyn then acquired Powys and moved south into Ceridigion, where he rebuilt Aberystwyth castle, but as happened to many overweening conquerors, his ambitions betrayed him. John attacked in 1211, drove him out of Rhos and Rhufoniog, crossed the Conwy (the only English king to do so for almost two hundred years) and burnt Bangor. Pressing south into Ceridigion he quelled the chiefs of that area and in turn built a new castle at Aberystwyth and another at Mathrafal, but the Welsh chiefs turned on him, and for two years not only the chiefs, but some of the marcher lords supported Llywelyn against John. The war that raged in the west spread across to the eastern March and into England, where Llywelyn captured Shrewsbury and the barons took London. In 1215, however, the *Magna Carta* ensured the king's peace and restored Welsh law to Wales. Llywelyn's position was at last secure and his control was restored over a wide area either by alliances and overlordship, or directly. There were treaties to be drawn up, difficulties and aggressions to come, but he was now firmly established as the ruler of a state run on near-feudal lines. Under Henry II, the title 'king' was no longer permitted to Welsh rulers, and until 1230 Llywelyn was known by the resounding title of 'prince of Aberffraw and lord of Snowdon'. He won the loyalty of those chiefs who acknowledged his overlordship, and brought independent Wales to the high point of her history, to be remembered by posterity as Llywelyn the Great.

Coffin of Llywelyn the Great, Llanrwst church

VIII Llywelyn and Edward

Llywelyn the Last

In the 9th century England and Wales were comparable politically in that both Rhodri and Alfred achieved the near union of several kingdoms. By the 12th century no such comparability existed. England had then been united for more than a hundred years firmly governed under a feudal system, and was administratively more advanced than any other country in the West. But independent Wales was divided into three major kingdoms and a number of lesser lordships, and her eastern and southern flank was part of the Marcher belt. Welsh society was still based on the tribe and the family, each *gwlad* looking inward except when it was in conflict with its neighbours. Welsh custom militated against political stability and union: such unity as there was being rooted in her language, laws, her way of life, and the Celtic Church. The economy especially of the more remote districts was that of a self-sufficing peasantry with no money to facilitate trade and exchange except in a few ports. Yet Gwynedd could boast a series of great kings from 1039, many of whom had contacts with the royal house and the barons of England and the Marches, and through these, English ideas had seeped in to affect Welsh life even before the 13th century. But her history depended to too great a degree on the character and achievements of her rulers, some weak, some strong. From the early 11th century Powys produced no major rulers, Deheubarth only one—the great Lord Rhys—while Gwynedd was ruled by no fewer than five outstanding men, reaching a high point under the two Princes, Llywelyn ap Iorwerth and Llywelyn ap Gruffydd. Known as Llywelyn the Last, grandson of Llywelyn the Great, Llywelyn ap Gruffydd's story was one of triumph and eventual misfortune: doomed to decline through disasters to tragedy.

From their early years in England the Normans had pursued an unremitting policy of bringing Wales into submission. Yet when the last Llywelyn's reign began, southern Britain was still very clearly tripartite, England, the Marches and independent Wales forming distinctive and contrasted political and cultural entities. It was demonstrated vividly during the reign of Stephen and again during the Barons' War of 1263. For two hundred years the independent Welsh kingdoms had been mutilated by the amputation of their country's eastern and southern flanks and constant conflict with England or the marcher lords or both. Llywelyn the Great came near to uniting free Wales, and the last Llywelyn staged a brilliant repetition only to witness his achievements collapse like a pack of cards during his final tragic years. From 1255 Llywelyn ruled alone, having imprisoned Owain and David, his two brothers, perhaps as a result of having absorbed the Norman concept of a single heir, as well as other feudal ideas such as centralised power, a hierarchical structure of society, the need to foster trade, improve production, and to shed many of the customs which were a drag on Welsh progress. From 1256–7 he strove to add vast new areas to his principality: all north-east Wales was conquered in that first year with the exception of Disserth and Degannwy castles. Driving Llywelyn ap Maredudd from Merioneth, he overran Ceridigion and turned south-east into the Mortimer country, taking many of his lands from that wealthy marcher lord; and thence into Powys in 1257. Midsummer of that year saw him extending his victorious passage into the south-west, capturing the south Carmarthenshire castles, and from there advancing into Glamorgan. With all Wales free, and parts of former Marcher Wales either his or paying homage to him, he awarded himself the proud title of Prince of Wales.

Relations with the king had been good on the whole, but even Henry III had a turning point. True, Henry's main interest was ecclesiastical architecture and he was far more interested in rebuilding St Edward's great church, the Westminster Abbey that we know today, than in Wales. But Llywelyn's challenge could no longer be ignored. In his last campaign Henry marched into North Wales from Chester, and recaptured Disserth and Degannwy, only to be forced to abandon them. A truce was called, and the trouble between Henry and the barons was soon to break into open war and call him back into England. Llywelyn seized the opportunity of sweeping into the southern Marches, retaking a number of castles, and with the help of his powerful ally, Simon de Montfort, was further successful in subduing some of its major strongpoints, notably Ludlow and Hereford. So it continued, but at the battle of Evesham the Welsh were defeated and Simon was slain. However, Llywelyn was still in so strong a position that he could go some way to negotiating his own terms, and historians agree that the *Treaty of Montgomery* of 1267 marked the peak of his career. His brother David had defected to Henry before the Barons' War, and the king now rewarded him with the restoration of his lost lands, but confirmed to Llywelyn his title of Prince of Wales. Thereafter there was to be only one king, and he on the English throne.

Troubles and problems mounted from that time. The long tide of success had turned and Llywelyn's relations with England worsened. Within 10 years, having inexplicably lost either his nerve or his former martial farsightedness, he was making mistake after mistake. His brother David must bear no small share in the responsibility for the reversal of events, having returned to the English court in 1274, and then it was no longer Henry, but his strong and able son, Edward I, who was on the throne. Wales was divided. Nevertheless, when the first war of Welsh Independence began, David returned to fight with the prince. The outcome measured the extent of Llywelyn's loss of status, when at its close the *Treaty of Aberconwy* (1277) stripped him of the homage of all the Welsh chiefs, and desperately reduced his hold on Wales. Refusing to pay homage to Edward, Eleanor de Montfort to whom the prince had been married by proxy, was detained in custody by the king. Llywelyn had failed to understand, it seems, the degree to which Edward's control had extended. He was fined heavily and at last forced to pay homage to Edward. The succession of his Principality which had been confirmed to Llywelyn's heirs by the *Treaty of Montgomery* (1267) was never to become reality. Even though the marriage was eventually solemnised with great pomp, and at Edward's expense in Worcester cathedral, the only child of the union was a daughter, Gwenllian. Eleanor, her mother, died in childbirth, and Edward gained possession of the infant, placing her in a convent which she never left.

Llywelyn the Last

The final act was due to David's rashness in initiating the Second War of Welsh Independence in 1282. Revolts broke out all over Wales and Llywelyn had little option but to support his brother, though the responsibility for its outbreak was not his. It is impossible to determine whose was the real responsibility for the conflict, Edward's, David's, or in the train of recent events, Llywelyn's. But once launched Edward gave no quarter in his determined progress towards the conquest of Wales and its anglicisation either during or after the war of 1282. The accidental discovery and assassination of the prince near Llanganten on the moors above Builth on 11 December 1282, and the dispatch of his head to Edward was the horror which ended his remarkable, yet tragic, story. David doggedly continued the revolt, but he was captured the following year and executed at Shrewsbury. There were no heirs, no royal line of Gwynedd, and in 1284 Edward drew up the terms of the *Statute of Rhuddlan* and master-minded the settlement which followed. The dream of a united and independent Wales had died with the death of its gallant prince.

IX Native Gwynedd and the Statute of Rhuddlan

In 1189, the year following the accession of Llywelyn the Great, the Archdeacon of Brecon and Gerald the Welshman (Giraldus Cambrensis) journeyed round Wales with Archbishop Baldwin of Canterbury. The *Itinerary of Wales* and *The Description of Wales* are the records of this journey written by Gerald. Only eight days were spent in North Wales, and topographical detail is scanty, but everything he wrote was the product of an acute observer's personal impressions, an invaluable record compiled towards the end of a century when the way of life in Wales had been altering slowly but surely. It was the threshold of the momentous 13th century. A hundred years after Archbishop Baldwin's tour the major revolution of the Edwardian settlement was under way, and 200 years of difficult adjustment were still to follow.

St Deinio's church, Pwllheli

Gerald was the son of a Norman nobleman, and his grandmother was the beautiful Nest, a Welsh princess married to Gerald of Windsor, and the daughter of Rhys ap Tewdwr, the last independent prince of South Wales. A son of one of the many Anglo-Welsh alliances, Gerald was fair minded, but at the same time passionately espoused the cause of his Welsh compatriots. Of Anglesey he wrote 'the island is incomparably more fertile than any other part of Wales', and he estimated that it could supply the entire country. Eryri, the mountains of Snowdonia, had such abundant pastures, he averred, 'that they could supply . . . all the herds of cattle in Wales'. But the land of the sons of Cynan (Merioneth) he deemed 'the roughest and rudest district of all Wales; the ridges of its mountains', he continued, 'are very high and narrow, terminating in sharp peaks, and . . . irregularly jumbled together'. His accounts of the people and their way of life are far more penetrating if by no means always complimentary, referring to their inconstancy and instability, their life of plunder and disregard of peace, their seizure of lands and dissension among brothers. But he is equally concerned to display their virtues as he saw them: boldness, courage, hospitality, liberality, quickness of understanding, wit and confidence in speech, and particular stress is laid on family links, their interest in genealogy, and their devotion to Christianity.

The overall picture is of a rustic life in which pastoralism was predominant, the people 'eating more flesh than bread', but a society which also had a strong warrior element. Cultivation was subsidiary,

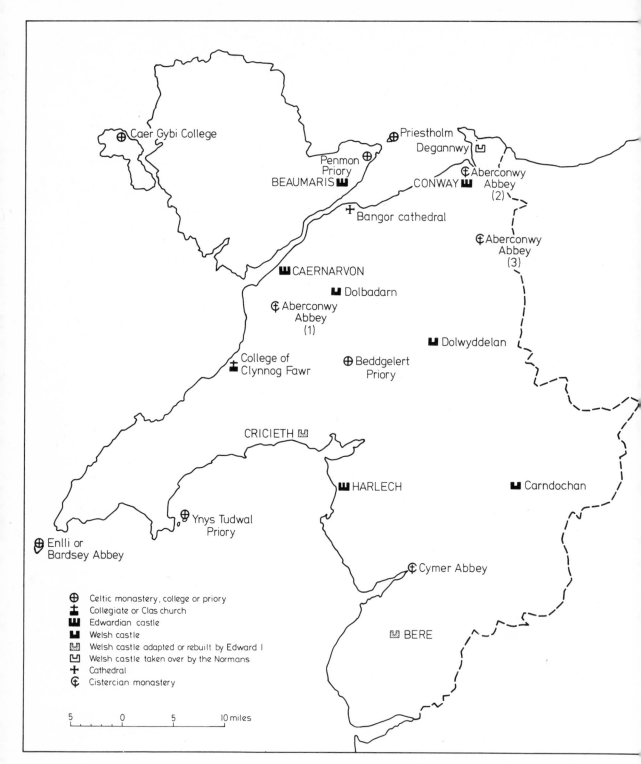

Caer Gybi College

Priestholm
Degannwy

Penmon
Priory

BEAUMARIS

CONWAY   Aberconwy
Abbey
(2)

Bangor cathedral

Aberconwy
Abbey
(3)

CAERNARVON

Dolbadarn

Aberconwy
Abbey
(1)

Dolwyddelan

College of
Clynnog Fawr

Beddgelert
Priory

CRICIETH

HARLECH

Carndochan

Ynys Tudwal
Priory

Enlli or
Bardsey Abbey

Cymer Abbey

BERE

⊕	Celtic monastery, college or priory
✚	Collegiate or Clas church
᠁	Edwardian castle
᠁	Welsh castle
᠁	Welsh castle adapted or rebuilt by Edward I
᠁	Welsh castle taken over by the Normans
✝	Cathedral
₵	Cistercian monastery

5   0   5   10 miles

Map 7. Medieval Castles and Religious Houses

but they used the plough with either two or four oxen, harvested with sickles, and had neither orchards nor gardens. Gathering, hunting, and fishing were part of the rural régime as land and opportunity afforded. 'They neither inhabit towns, villages, or castles . . . but content themselves with small huts made of the boughs of trees twisted together'. However, Gerald was writing towards the end of a century during which, in fact, the proportion of bondmen in the population was lessening, and tillage becoming more important in fields held in common.

Cymer Abbey

When Llywelyn the Great first succeeded to the throne of Gwynedd, conditions were as Gerald described them. Tribalism still meant the blood feud: justice in the hands of the kindred. It meant the existence of isolated family groups, the *gweliau*, and the progressive morcellation of their holdings because of equal partition among a man's heirs, and other survivals of an outdated system to which a sparse population in lonely holdings clung by tradition. The contrast with conditions in England was widening, but very slowly the stability of a firm centralised administration and legal system had been influencing sections of Welsh opinion as the 12th century advanced.

Llywelyn the Great set out deliberately to modernise the structure of his realm, not only Gwynedd but the other *gwledydd* of which he was overlord, and whose chieftains he insisted should pay homage to him. He fought the blind conservatism of tribal practice, and revised the laws of Hywel Dda. Working with his lawyers and the remarkable and able Ednyfed Fychan, his seneschal, he made the individual rather than the *gwely* responsible for criminal and other illegal acts, reforms which were to continue under his grandson. During the 13th century, the standard of life and advancement of the economy were taking place at an increasing pace. A few market centres arose, small and inconsiderable at first, near the Norman castles and the little ports. Life became more settled as tillage increased in proportion to pastoralism, and the local chiefs at least began to build better dwellings. Money seeped into commerce as trade swelled in the ports and markets, not in a spectacular way, but as a gently gathering tide. The late Professor T. Jones Pierce suggested that many of the more permanent rural centres that we see in Wales today originated then, that local boundaries became defined, and the older locality names gave place to new.

The Church, which had accepted the rule of Rome in 768 and the authority of Canterbury during the early Norman period, was also changing in some respects. Diocesan organisation was one such field. The early bishops in Wales had little or no part in diocesan matters, and there is no record of the origin of Bangor diocese. It is thought

The Dovecote, Penmon

unlikely that it goes back to the time of Deiniol, its first bishop and founder, but it must be presumed to have been before 768. Another change related to the monastic houses. Some of the more isolated, such as Priestholm (Ynys Seiriol) had found their poverty and remoteness too great, the brothers returning to Penmon or simply not being replaced by new recruits at death. But others better placed had come into the regular orders, particularly that of the Cistercians who were popular with the Welsh. The abbey at Aberconwy was founded in 1186 when Cistercian monks from Strata Florida chose a site a few miles from Caernarvon at Rhedynog Felen, moving to the Conwy estuary at some time prior to 1192, Llywelyn making them magnificent grants of land and according numerous privileges. They had been there for less than a hundred years when, in 1283, Edward chartered the new borough of Conway and the planned town with its massive castle were to take precedence. None of the conventual buildings remains, only the great church. The abbey removed to the Conwy valley some little distance below Llanrwst, and remained there at Maenan until its dissolution in 1537. Many of the early Celtic churches, so numerous in Gwynedd's countryside, were being rebuilt at this time, some of them only simple rectangular stone erections such as still are far from untypical, others displaying the results of effective contacts with England where ecclesiastical architecture was in the graceful and beautiful Early English and Transitional phase. This process continued as and when money was available, or a rich patron was prepared to cover the cost, but some early characteristics, such as the double aisle and double entrance persisted in many, while others were designed on the lines familiar in England and on the Continent at the time. Another community which had terminated was that at Clynnog which became a *clas,* a mingling of a collegiate and a mother church. Aberdaron was also a *clas.* In Merioneth, at the invitation of local chieftains, Cistercians from Abbey Cwm Hir (Radnorshire) established Cymer abbey in the parish of Llanelltyd, and it, too, was chartered by Llywelyn the Great. With their tradition of sheep-rearing this Order was popular with the Welsh. The Church had always had an important place in the Norman scheme of things, and rich endowments were bestowed on it in Gwynedd by Llywelyn ap Iorwerth and Llywelyn ap Gruffydd, and after the Conquest. Prior to the Dissolution of the monasteries these church lands were very extensive indeed, notably in Caernarvonshire. In the mid-12th century all four Welsh bishoprics were in the fold of Canterbury. It had been very much against the wishes of the princes of Gwynedd, as it was also of Gerald's, but in the 13th century it was seen that some of the results at least were favourable, and it had beome part of the established order.

Such was the background picture in the time of the two Llywelyns. Both the state of the country and the events which led to Gwynedd's final submission, as described in the previous chapter, left Edward I with no easy task. Llywelyn ap Gruffydd's dream of a united independent Wales in association with England was what he and his grandfather had so long worked to achieve. In 1267 it had seemed to take shape on a not-too-distant horizon, but all these hopes lay shattered before the end of 1282 when Llywelyn's body lay broken on the bleak winter moorland above Builth. But he had throughout recognized the advantages of the more modern régime operative in England.

Since 1277, the Cardigan-Carmarthen area, centred on the castellaries first established by Henry III, had become an accretion of further territorial acquisitions, and they were ruled, not as true shires, but as honour-counties administered by the Crown. In 1284 under the provisions of the Statute of Rhuddlan they became jointly the Principality of South Wales, to be administered as the shires of Cardigan and Carmarthen. The *cantrefi* of Rhos and Rhufoniog, the country between the Conwy and the Clwyd, so long wrangled over by Gwynedd and England, were bestowed on the earl of Lincoln as the lordship of Denbigh. To the south-east Dyffryn Clwyd and the *gwlad* of Powys Fadog were sub-divided to form a string of smaller lordships which completed the long crescent of the Marches extending from the mid-north coast of Wales to its south-western tip.

13th-century font, Llanrhuychwyn

Gwynedd itself was now completely flanked by these lordships except at the Dyfi estuary, and in 1284 it was constituted the Principality of North Wales. As far as Gwynedd was concerned the war dragged on into 1284, but with little real success, and with the capture and execution of David it was all over. Yet the country was in a state of unrest and much of that year was taken up with attempts to subdue the scattered outbreaks of trouble. It took still longer to solve the mountain of problems which Edward's victory had brought to him, and Gwynedd posed the most challenging of these. His solution was to divide it into shires like the English counties, but with a very different administrative set-up. The boundaries had first to be decided. Anglesey offered no difficulty; it is a natural unit. Mainland Gwynedd was less simple, and the first proposal was to create a northern county consisting of the commote of Creuddyn and the two *cantrefi* of Arllechwedd and Arfon, to be called Aberconwyshire; and the *cantrefi* of Llŷn and Dunoding, i.e., southern portions of the later counties of Caernarvonshire and northern Merioneth, together to form a county of Cricieth. By 1284, this scheme had been abandoned in favour of Caernarvonshire as it remained until 1974, and a third county, Merioneth, extending to the Dyfi estuary.

St Hywyn's church,
Aberdaron

The new and elaborate administrative plans for this Principality were keyed under the Statute of Rhuddlan to the creation of castellated boroughs populated by English officials and burgesses. Central points of this type had long operated in the marcher lordships. From as early as 1283, the building of the great Edwardian castles was already under way and new towns planned on the selected sites. Some, like Harlech, Cricieth, and Caernarvon were on pre-existing Welsh castle sites, but were either massive new constructions or extensively added to. But one of three major new boroughs in Caernarvonshire had no such early Welsh forerunner: Conway was selected instead of the ancient site of Degannwy across the estuary which had been occupied from the Dark Ages, and which was the traditional seat of Maelgwn Gwynedd. Later again, this had been replaced by a Norman castle, but to the Edwardians a close link with the sea was essential. The associated boroughs were chartered: Caernarvon and Conway in 1284, Cricieth, Bere, and Harlech in 1285. Following these early planned towns, a serious revolt broke out in Anglesey led by one Madoc ap Llywelyn and as a result two boroughs were chartered in the island, Beaumaris in 1295 and Newborough in 1303. All these were royal boroughs and their charters based on that of Hereford which in turn had been modelled on Breteuil and its famous laws. Huge sums of money and large armies of workmen were used in their creation which involved not only the great bastide-type fortresses but houses for officials and burgesses, the erection of walls round some of the towns, the construction or repair of quays, docks, and bridges in others, all essential not only for defence and communication, but for the victualling of the people concerned and the transportation of building materials. Every town was an Edwardian island within the wide rural lands of Gwynedd which lay beyond, and where the population was predominantly agricultural and Welsh. Later again, three free boroughs, perhaps on the sites of earlier Welsh settlements, were chartered at Nefyn, Pwllheli, and Bala, and administered by a mayor and bailiffs, not by the constable of a castle. They had the privilege of forming gilds merchant, and it was into these that Welsh burgesses filtered and eventually were able to conduct self government.

The administrative structure was characteristically hierarchical, centralised on Caernarvon for the Principality, and the three component shires, each having its own sheriff, justice, chamberlain, and chancellor. In this field also, Edward was a skilled planner, blending English with customary Welsh law, English predominating notably in the matter of the criminal law. This combination made for judicial progress and modernisation, but displayed the wisdom of retaining sound traditional and customary roots. *Rhagliaid,* resident officials responsible for the commotes (which were retained as local administrative units), were supported by a *rhyngyll* or reeve, and a peace-keeping body of men who were in essence police. The revised criminal law, transferring offences against the kindred to offences against the state, and foreshadowed by the reforms of the two Llywelyns, was of fundamental importance for the keeping of the king's peace as well as affording a drastic reconception of liability for ill-doing. Under civil provisions numerous new laws were introduced, notably the change in the laws of inheritance from gavelkind (equal division of the patrimony between heirs) to primogeniture. But if a villein died without heirs, the king could still seize his land as the princes had done in the pre-Conquest period. A succession of courts from the Great Sessions, through the county courts to the hundred courts dealt with pleas, offences, and other legal matters. In addition, the Sheriff's Turn which dealt with changes in the law, was held twice a year, and attendance was compulsory for all landowners except men of religion, clerks, and women. The exemption of the religious community indicated its distinction in status and in law, and Edward's generosity to and protection of the Church was in line with a policy established from the beginning of the Norman period. Henceforward in Wales also, the Church was to be an inherent part of the structure of the state as it was in feudal England, and some acceleration of church rebuilding bore witness to this. In Western Europe ecclesiastical architecture was passing through and into its finest centuries, and in Wales as in England, rebuilt churches displayed Continental influence.

Edward's victory had extinguished the hopes of a united and independent Wales nurtured by Llywelyn ap Iorwerth and Llywelyn ap Gruffydd and towards which they had striven for so long. But in matters of administration the Statute of Rhuddlan ushered in a new area. More immediately many, though by no means all, Welshmen were conscious of advantages and disadvantages. Very few offices were held by them in the first decade or so, and exclusion from the castellated boroughs was almost total. The results of the stimulus to output and trade, for instance, could not immediately be envisaged, but the scene was irreversibly set for the next two hundred years, and Wales became progressively more like England in its economy and administration. Poets and prophets prayed for the rise of a Welsh saviour, but none could then have foreseen that victory, on a remote English field, which sealed the fate of the Lancastrians and brought the first Henry Tudor, a Welsh-speaking Welshman, to the throne of England.

X Castles and Castle Towns

From the time of the Conquest, Norman and Plantagenet kings planted new towns with strong defences in England and, as they advanced into eastern and southern Wales and into the Marcher lordships, they established them there also. In some, natural defences were strengthened, rivers crossed by defended bridges, hills topped with wooden or stone castles, and towns walled. From the mid-13th century, Henry III was pursuing a similar policy, and planting many strong 'bastides' in his lands in Gascony. The bastides represented a marked advance in design as against the comparatively simple early Norman fortresses and other defences. Towns were equipped with high walls, strongly defended gates, elaborate castles in which defences were no longer focused on towers but on curtain walls, these and other features all calculated to withstand the most vigorous siege methods employed in an age of widespread war. When Edward I succeeded to the throne of England and thereby also acquired Henry's French possessions, he had copy book examples of these new plantations and a master architect in James de St George.

After the fall of Gwynedd, Edward got to work on his new North Welsh domains with typical vigour. From 13 March to 9 May 1283 he took up quarters in Aberconwy Abbey, then a solitary group of conventual buildings on the west bank of the Conwy estuary near the age-old ferry crossing. The Welsh castle of Degannwy occupied the heights on the opposite bank, and the Iron Age hill fort towered above the abbey to the west, but Edward immediately recognized the value of Conway as the gateway to Gwynedd. It was then a land which could boast few settlements larger than a small cluster, such as groups near to a harbour, or an inland trading point which rarely had even an organized market. The Marches were the only part of Wales where, at that time, the Normans had introduced new castellated boroughs. Gwynedd, lying outside the Marches, and so long the last bastion of Welsh independence, knew no such introductions. So Edward, following up the Statute of Rhuddlan, made all speed to support the new administrative structure by founding castle towns.

Gwynedd's remoteness made the country both more difficult to defend and more vital to keep securely under English control. Such is its mountainous character that wide areas are unattractive to settlements of any size while its coasts cry out for urban development and

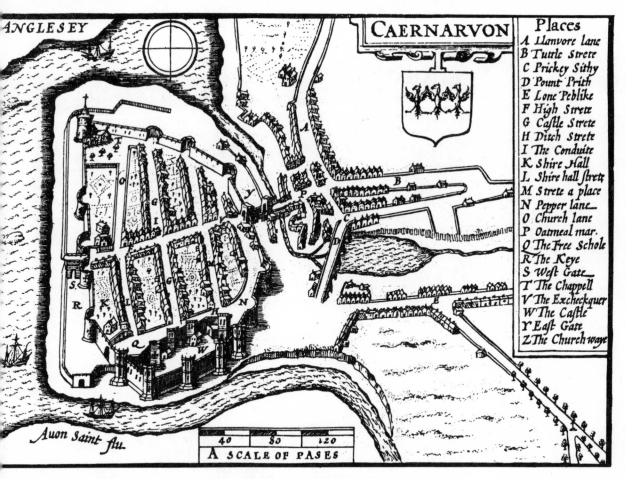

ANGLESEY

CAERNARVON

Auon Saint flu.

40   80   120

A SCALE OF PASES

Map 8.—Plan of Caernarvon, John Speed, 1610.

trade, and in those days they needed defence against raiders. Edward's royal progress through Caernarvonshire in 1284 is well known, and he must have planned castles and associated boroughs to be sited at Conway, Caernarvon, and Harlech during his earlier stay at Conway Abbey, for work began on each of these three castles in that year. In addition he took over the Welsh castles of Cricieth and Bere (Caerberllan), and adapted them. The first four were all on coastal sites, with harbours, and were valuable as lookouts. Llywelyn ap Iorwerth's castle at Bere had no such advantages and was soon abandoned, but it is of especial interest as the most extensive of the princes' castles. Beaumaris, however, in 1294 was to become the fifth of the Edwardian castle towns of Gwynedd, following revolts in the island as a result of an uprising sponsored by one Madog ap Llywelyn.

At first sight primarily a conqueror, Edward was, in fact, a brilliant and far-sighted strategist, administrator, and planner, as skilled in imposing the 1284 Settlement as he had been in conducting his wars.

61

Centuries of close links between the monarchy and the countries of Western Christendom had resulted in England being far more advanced in its economy than Wales, and to bring his newly-conquered territory into its orbit, he created the castellated boroughs of North Wales across the entire width of the country, initiating a revolution in the landscape, the economy and society alike.

Conway was and has remained the proud gateway to Snowdonia, affording access to the far western coastlands, and to Anglesey across the Menai Straits. The abbey complex was formerly the only settlement on the otherwise deserted western shores of the Conwy estuary, and Edward re-sited it at Maenan further up the valley, only the abbey church remaining when the conventual buildings were razed to the ground to make way for the new town. Even their exact site is uncertain though it is thought that they extended from the church to near the foot of castle hill. This hill is a low ridge of Silurian sandstone and gritstone overlooking both the estuary and the lesser Gyffin valley. It lies within a comparatively level stretch of Ordovician mudstones and there the town was constructed within the triangular town walls, now a monument unparalleled in Britain. To the north behind the long wall which follows the estuarine shore, over 700 acres were earmarked for the town itself. The entire intra-mural town and its castle were built together, and a garrison of 30 maintained from 1284. The massive new fortress on its rocky eminence, now somewhat dwarfed by subsequent changes in road and bridge construction, cost between £15,000 and £20,000 to build, each £1,000 the equivalent of about £1,000,000 today. Its chief designer was Master de St George and the workmen were numbered in hundreds. European defensive architecture having moved away from the earlier emphasis on a strong keep to the elaboration of curtain walls, those at Conway had to be adapted to the elongated site on the rock. They enclose two baileys, and eight circular towers project outwards from the walls. Strong barbicans at each end, west and east, take the place of gatehouses, that at the west end giving access from the town. The western barbican is nearer to the royal living quarters, the king's hall and chamber built within the south curtain, and the chapel tower occupies the north-east angle of the walls. In the larger outer bailey the great hall is built on to the south curtain; the household quarters on the north with the well (or reservoir) adjacent.

As E. A. Lewis stressed, the protection of Gwynedd's castle towns was of national as well as local importance, for invasions by Scots and Irish were not unknown, and there was even the possibility of French landings. Hence the town walls were an integral part of the total plan. They, too, were at first maintained by the Crown, though murage was paid by all bringing vendable goods to the weekly Tuesday market.

Later the townsfolk were made responsible for the upkeep of the walls, and it seems that they were glad to do so for their own safety's sake in those troubled times. Markets and fairs were held near to the castle. For the rest, the main street plan consisted of routes linking up the four town gates. Narrower ways were only added when the population increased in Tudor and later periods. The constable of the castle, together with other officers such as the chaplain, treasurer, and gaoler, garrison and armourer, household and maintenance staff, were resident either in the castle or the town, and there were also various tradesmen and burgesses residing in the town. Such was a typical set-up in the castle towns, where mills, workshops, storehouses and other buildings and their stewards must all be provided. The borough or castle mills were particularly important, as were supplies of other food, and the victualling of the castle was a prime requirement. Much of it was available from the nearby countryside, for behind Conway lies the fertile if narrow ribbon of the lower Conwy valley, to the south and west the almost unlimited pastures of Snowdonia, and to the north Gwynedd's traditional granary of Anglesey. In addition, the land between the main streets of the early town provided the burgage land, another source of fresh food, and there were river and sea fisheries nearby. The charter of 1284 granted annual fairs and a weekly Tuesday market. For rarer foods and wines, fine cloths and Continental manufactures such as swords, jewellery, and various luxury goods, the port was at hand for both coastwise vessels and foreign shipping.

Town walls and Menai shore, Caernarvon

Caernarvon controlled the western approaches of the Menai Straits, and the importance of its strategically significant site had been recognised from Roman times. Edward selected it equally unerringly as the administrative centre for the entire North Wales Principality, and here were held both the Great Sessions and the Caernarvonshire shire court. Here, too, resided all the officials associated with the central functions of its chief town. At the junction of the north and west coast roads of Wales, Caernarvon also commanded the lesser tracks into the Llŷn peninsula and into the heart of Snowdonia, and had immediate access to south-west Anglesey across the waters of Menai. Victualling offered no problems unless in times of siege, nor did the importation of foreign goods. But the question of defence was paramount on this flat site with admirable land and sea communications. A motte already existed on the site of the present castle, thought to have been raised by Hugh of Chester in the late 11th century, but possibly by the Welsh, who certainly had a *llys* here from some time in the 12th century. This was adequately defensible, but the new town was not, and priority in the Edwardian building programme was the construction of a town wall to protect the entire settlement. This was completed between 1283 and 1285. As in Conway, the town was roughly bisected by its High Street, from which a few lesser streets crossed between walls and the Town Ditch. Beyond the Ditch the castle was completed much more slowly. It was built in three stages, the last only completed in 1322. The area of the town was double that of Conway, and the castle is more magnificent, and its walls much stronger. The ground plan of the two castles is similar, Caernarvon's castle being an elongated structure built round two baileys. Its two great gates (King's and Queen's) opened the one across the (then deep) moat known as the Town Ditch, the other on to the open square at high level. The masons' techniques alone would distinguish this from any other Edwardian castle in North Wales. Most of the stone is Carboniferous Limestone, probably from Penmon, and is contrasted with granite from nearby Twt Hill, and the warm tones of Triassic sandstone from Cheshire or perhaps from the ruined fort of *Segontium*. The polychrome effect is enhanced by the dressing of the stone and the regular courses; and the multi-angular towers look quite different from the round towers of the other castles. The immediate rock surface on which the castle stands was in part insufficiently strong to bear its great weight, so it was underpinned to stronger rock beds deep below the foundations. The walls are exceptionally thick, those on the south curtain being pierced by two galleries which give easy and rapid access from Queen's Tower on the south-west corner to Queen's Gate at the west end, an invaluable device both in peace and war. There are seven large towers in the curtain, chambers, and a smaller prison tower in the King's Gate which is strictly a gatehouse. Other buildings divided the two baileys, and in the inner bailey were the great hall and the kitchens, these last adjacent to the Well Tower. Eagle Tower with two slender inner towers rising above the main structure is the most striking, but its function, as that which is nearest to the Anglesey shore and the western entrance to the Straits, is more than ornamental, for its great height affords an exceptionally broad field of view. Caernarvon has deservedly been described as one of the finest castles in Britain and even in Western Europe.

Harlech, the third of the castles which Edward began to build in 1283, was in many ways different from the two north coast castle towns. Occupying a steep rocky spur on the Harlech Dome, which drops sharply to the sea in northern Merioneth, this massive four-square fortress gives a visual impression of strength unrivalled in Gwynedd. Erected between 1283 and 1290, its defences were increased from 1295 by an embattled wall to the west leading down to 'Gate next the Sea', the total cost amounting to over £8,200. In plan it is an approximate square, and represents the transition to the concentric castle more fully developed at Beaumaris. Standing some 200 feet above the sea,

North gateway of Harlech Castle

22. (*above left*) Cricieth castle seen from Dinas and showing the low outer wall and foundations of two of the Welsh towers. The Edwardian building is within the Welsh wall.

23. (*above*) Cricieth castle from the east side showing the Edwardian towers dominating the scene.

24. (*left*) Gwydir castle; a drawing by Charles Tunnicliffe, R.A.

25.   Baron Hill, near Beaumaris: the home of the Bulkeleys rebuilt by the 7th Lord Bulkeley. Samuel Wyatt was the architect.

27.   Llangian (Llŷn peninsula); cottages clearly marking two stages in the evolution of the Welsh house.

26.   Llanrwst Bridge: a drawing by Charles Tunnicliffe, R.A.

28.   Amlwch harbour, Anglesey.

29. Conway's bridges seen from the castle in the 1950s.

30. Penmaenmawr. The narrow ledge used by the coast road and the pier from which granite is shipped.

31. The Sychnant Pass, once the main route from Conway westward along the north coast.

it surmounts in grandeur a hill consisting of tough grits and sandstones, similar to those of the nearby quarries from which the castle building stone was quarried, and the jointed rocks of which yield springs to supply water *in situ.* From its superb situation, it commands a wide stretch of country, including the entire length of Llŷn to the west, and a long vista of Cardigan Bay and its coastlands to the south. The sea is thought to have come appreciably nearer to the foot of the castle hill when it was built, and a dock once existed at the end of an embattled wall extending from the south-western tower to 'Gate next the Sea', now some distance from the shore. Its military strength was such that it remained a maiden fortress, but its disadvantages were its limited port facilities and its ill-populated mountain hinterland where agriculture was virtually limited to pastoralism with the minimum of crop raising. Its borough housed in 1294 a population of only 34 with a garrison in the castle of under thirty men. But, lying on a coastal route (though not the main Roman road) south, and in the rather remote southern shire of this North Wales Principality, it had self-evident strategic value. By contrast, the site of the few dwellings which house the townsfolk was anything but satisfactory, as today's sharply different levels show. Unwalled and unplanned, it was in total contrast with Caernarvon and Conway; there was never the insistence on the townsfolk being English, and its market was always poor.

Across Tremadoc Bay within easy signalling distance lay Edward's fourth castle, **Cricieth.** It had become a royal Welsh residence about 1230, when, according to C. A. Gresham's study of the history of Cricieth, they deserted Dolbenmaen three miles to the north, the former administrative centre of Eifionydd, and built a castle in the then bond township of Tre Ferthyr, which was to be renamed Cricieth. The castle stands on a steep little hill of igneous rock (felsite) just over 100 feet in height, which falls sheer to the sea on the south. There was a small landing place east of the castle, but if it operated as a port it seems to have been a very minor one and it probably depended on local rather than imported supplies. As a fortress, it was of secondary strategic importance, but it completed Edward's mainland chain of coastal castles. It

Cricieth Castle

is the only one of the four Edwardian mainland castles which combines both Edwardian and earlier Welsh masonry. The inner ward is of irregular shape, small, and with the principal rooms assumed to have been in the gatehouse. The Cistern Tower was the work of Edwardian masons. A borough was chartered here also in 1284 with a weekly market, but it was not a walled town and must have been exceptionally small, though it had its garrison and English burgesses. Dr. Gresham assumes that the Edwardian settlement was clustered on either side of castle hill, and this nucleus became known as *Y Dref* or *Yr Hen Dref.*

Edward's original fifth choice was **Bere**, also near to another of Llywelyn's residences, but its inland location in a mountainous ill-populated countryside was soon to prove it a poor selection, and although it was chartered as a borough, and the castle—a Welsh structure—was the largest and most up-to-date native fortress in Gwynedd, it was soon abandoned. Indeed, its exact location became a matter for conjecture, but excavations and the clearing of the site have revealed its ruins and recently have produced interesting finds. The puzzle is why Edward ever chose it for a borough? Was it because it had a strong existing fortress? Or because it could serve as a link with Ceredigion?

In the event, therefore, it was **Beaumaris** which became Edward's permanent fifth stronghold. Begun some eleven years later than those he first planned, all of which were on the mainland, the decision to fortify a site in Anglesey was consequential on the revolt led by Madog ap Llywelyn which brought to a head a state of unrest in the island. Characteristically, nothing was permitted to stand in the way when Edward decided to plan the new castle and borough, partly in Llanfaes and partly in Cerrig-y-Gwyddell, in a neighbouring *tref*. The dwellings of the two *trefydd* were in his way, and the entire population of Llanfaes was evacuated and re-settled in the extreme south-west of the island of Rhosfair, then a fertile district. But as the centuries passed south-westerly gales shifted sand inland, and the dunes encroached to form the now extensive Newborough Warren. To the north lay the marshes of the Malltraeth depression with similarly restricting effects on the prosperity of the new settlement of Newborough in the subsequent period. Beaumaris itself, founded and named anew, was on the edge of the Straits and barely above sea level. Llanfaes may already have been a ferrying point—now Beaumaris was to become both a ferry terminus and a port. The castle's local and foreign imports were ensured by a dock at its gates, and there were unloaded French wines, beautiful fabrics, toiletries, and furniture, as well as more mundane supplies, such as food and Spanish iron. The level land made possible the construction of a concentric castle of perfect symmetry, and unlike Harlech the outer curtain was of appreciable height. It was surrounded by a moat, still surviving as such on the north, west, and half of the southern perimeter of the curtain walls. It now ends at the old dock. Some kind of town wall was designed to contain the new borough, though a masonry wall was not completed until the early 15th century. Now only fragments remain, and much of its course is uncertain. As time passed, the sea built up a broad stretch of level land in front of the castle. It is known as the Green, but it in no way detracted from Beaumaris's growing prosperity as a ferry point, fishing centre, and port.

It is evident from the plans of castles such as Cricieth and Dolbadarn in particular, that the two Llywelyns had developed their military architecture during the 12th and 13th centuries. The design of those two castles was strikingly similar, each based on an irregularly-shaped curtain wall with rectangular towers. Dolwyddelan also had a curtain and rectangular towers, but is much smaller, and it is clear that Cricieth and Dolbadarn had better facilities as royal residences. Bere is elongated, sited on a precipitous narrow ridge, and has no projecting rectangular towers, but one circular and two U-shaped ones. Carndochan, near Bala, is somewhat similar, but much smaller. The contrast between Llywelyn I and II's defensive planning and that of Edward is of the greatest significance not only historically, but in relation to the changing geography of Gwynedd. The two Llywelyns had gone some considerable way towards achieving a well-defended feudal state, with the unification of a free Wales as their ultimate goal. But their strategy was purely defensive in relation to England, and the siting of their castles with the exception of Cricieth was planned as a ring round the mountain heart of Snowdon, and all too clearly designed for retreat rather than advance. None of their castles was associated in settlement terms with anything more than a rural manor.

By contrast, Edward not only built greater castles of advanced military design, but placed them on the sea coasts at points of both strategic and economic potential. The associated boroughs, especially in the case of the three northern ones embodied the foresight of an administrator who envisaged a developing modern commercialism and the transformation of a tribal society and economy. At the same time, the strength of his castles and his new administration spelt out unmistakably that his first goal was control of this recently-acquired territory and its people. The anglicisation of the boroughs was undoubtedly resented; nevertheless, there were to be many Welsh who sought appointments as officers in the new Gwynedd. As time passed English merchant families and officials mingled with Welshmen in the population of the castellated towns, and new predominantly Welsh boroughs and markets were created.

The Edwardian settlement had launched nothing less than a revolution, and though troubles and resentments were a-plenty, slowly it came to be recognised as the beneficial restructuring that was intended.

XI From Rhuddlan to the Union

Medieval knight's effigy, Tywyn church

Two hundred years separated the Edwardian Settlement from the accession of Henry Tudor after the Lancastrian victory on the field of Bosworth in 1485, years fraught with difficulties. Another half-century was to elapse before the Act of Union of England and Wales in 1536, but from Bosworth onwards there was light on the horizon, and slowly the formative influences began to be felt in social and economic life and in the landscape. For the first 200 years. however, unrest, rebellion, wars, and plague bedevilled life in Gwynedd, rising starkly from a background of unease and dissension. These varied ills were in part an unwilling adjustment to the political realities imposed by the enactment of the Statute of Rhuddlan, in part due to the general unrest and disease which were endemic in Western Europe in the 14th century. Gwynedd itself was faced with an entirely new administration abruptly superimposed on a rural and tribal society with its own deep-rooted traditions. Not only was it too sudden: it was seen only as the bitter fruit of conquest. Lowland Britain, unlike Gwynedd, had experienced the trauma of three major periods of conquest and extensive settlement since the Roman withdrawal— Anglo-Saxon, Scandinavian, and Norman. The eastern March had known 200 years of Norman takeover following on the earlier Anglo-Saxon and Roman extensions of overlordship which affected portions of that belt. All South Wales had been carved up into marcher lordships and forced into submission by these same Normans. In contrast, Gwynedd though raided and even invaded, had undergone no such wholesale occupations for 900 years; no control by an external conqueror since the withdrawal of Rome; and Rome had left the Celtic roots virtually undisturbed. It is not surprising that Gwynedd showed no readiness to accept new laws and administrators or to absorb a new Normanised urban element.

So resistance, revolt, and actual rebellion flared, and the sun was to set for many decades before there was anything approaching general recognition that beyond the immediate problems the seeds had been sown which could bear rewarding fruits. On the positive side there were the ingredients for development in the shape of new towns, enhanced trading prospects, transition to a money economy and, not least, a stable administration which embodied many of the features the two Llywelyns had been working to achieve. These last included

68

a (then) modern feudal structure towards which the princes had gone no small way. True, feudalism was by the 14th century nearing the latter phases of its dominance, with Simon de Montfort already pressing the issue of constitutionalism in England.

Town life in England after the Roman period was revived by both the Anglo-Saxons and the Scandinavians. When still larger numbers of these towns were planted in England and the Marches by the Normans in the late 11th and 12th centuries, and in turn by the Plantagenets, Gwynedd had no place deserving the name town. It was 1283 which marked the initiation of these urban foundations. Prior to this Degannwy was chartered as a borough by Henry III in 1252, but little has been discovered on the ground to suggest the erection of houses.

St Buan's church, Bodfean

The founding of Edward I's castellated boroughs drew a precise line to mark the real beginning of Gwynedd's urban history. An entirely new element was introduced into its geography in 1283-4, and, although they may appear to be primarily the most impressive monuments of the feudal age in its countryside, these castle towns were far more than that. They carried within them the seed of a long social and economic future in the case of Caernarvon, Conway, and Beaumaris and, together with Bangor, were to continue as important administrative centres. Harlech and Cricieth were of comparatively minor importance in the economic life of the region, but the location of the three sited on the Menaian shore was to prove Edward's far-sightedness. Neither Cricieth nor Harlech had good harbourage, both were away from the major trade routes, and Bere (Caerberllan) was a failed attempt to initiate a borough based on an existing Welsh stronghold situated in upland country difficult of access.

Four early Welsh boroughs were also created: that of Newborough has already been referred to as a re-settlement of the population of Llanfaes to clear the site for Beaumaris. Two small fishing ports in the Llŷn Peninsula, Nefyn on the north coast, and Pwllheli on the southern, were both chartered about 1284. They were Welsh from the outset and remained so, and developed a considerable early trade in fish. Newborough maintained a cattle trade with some success until the encroachment of sand from the dunes of Newborough Warren halted its growth. The fourth of the new Welsh towns, Bala, seems to have been created on a completely new site carved out of Llanycil parish and, as in the case of many other planted towns, its parish church lay outside its boundaries. Situated in the Dee valley where the river emerges from Llyn Tegid (Bala Lake), it became quietly successful as the centre for an agricultural area. So a total of nine of the Edwardian boroughs, together with the ancient ecclesiastical centre of Bangor, continued to focus and to foster the commercial life of Gwynedd for long years to come.

The centuries between the Statute of Rhuddlan and the Act of Union were rich with change in the political and intellectual life of England, but on the hard ground of rural Gwynedd, the sense of remoteness had grown in the aftermath of 1284, fostered, not least, by resentment against many of the provisions of the Settlement. Nevertheless, what was happening among the leaders of English thought and in certain sections of English society exerted an increasing influence on the Welsh gentry and the growing number of prosperous professional men and even merchants, as intermarriage became quite usual with the daughters of English families of corresponding status, and as more sons of well-to-do Gwynedd houses sent their sons to be educated in England. Welsh clerics and intending lawyers were among the early students at Oxford. From that time onward the trickle of Welsh into English schools, universities, and in due course into the Inns of Court, swelled to a river. The rising class of Welsh who were seeking positions at court, and the increasing numbers of scholars in touch with English learning and legal practice were fertile soil for the seeding of more advanced ideas in the fields of law, and indeed of commerce and religion. In this environment had developed a unique and rich culture, the flower of a rural and tribal society expressed by its bards and poets, in song, prose, and verse. In addition the Church played a dominant rôle in daily and seasonal life through its priesthood, its sacraments, and its festivals, as well as taking scholarship and the arts under its wing and being responsible for such education as was then available for the masses. In 1107, Llandaff accepted the authority of Canterbury and the remaining three dioceses followed later, including Bangor, which proclaimed its obedience to Rome by the middle of the century, albeit reluctantly. The princes of Gwynedd resisted this strongly, looking on the diocese as peculiarly their own. Further resentments inevitably followed when church endowments were taken over, *clasau* such as Clynnog Fawr suppressed, and celibacy of the priesthood imposed on unwilling clergy many of whom in the Welsh Church had taken wives. In addition, a new ecclesiastical geography was introduced in the shape of archdeaconries, rural deaneries, and parishes, each given precisely-defined boundaries.

13th-century pilgrim

The Welsh of Gwynedd had little use for such territorial organisation by the Church. By the mid-14th century its rôle in daily life had shrunk and the religious orders were in decline. A further shock and much genuine hardship were caused by the switch to a fiscal economy. Wide ranging fines and money rentals and taxes replaced the traditional dues. Peasants living on a hand-to-mouth economy simply had not the means to pay. Hence flocks and herds were either sold or confiscated. Many were rendered destitute or, at best, debts mounted. Harsh laws

70

such as the compulsory attendance at certain courts aroused objections, but the training it gave in administrative methods was later to prove of value to the many who sought office or determined on a legal career. The sorest of all grievances was perhaps the rigid exclusion of Welshmen from Conway, Caernarvon, and Beaumaris, the most prosperous of the new castellated towns, an exclusion long continued.

The upshot was a seething resentment which grew and was nurtured by contemporary bards and poets who revived the ancient prophecy that Arthur would one day return as king to redeem his people from a 'foreign' yoke. Indignation and deprivation were further increased by the introduction of the still more punitive Lancastrian penal code by Henry IV, the former Bolingbroke, first of the Lancastrian kings, at the opening of the 15th century. It excluded Welshmen even more rigidly from the boroughs, from a wide range of offices, and went so far as to forbid marriage between Welsh and English. Henry was seen as a monster and, as happens at times of crisis, a man of the moment materialised in the shape of Owain Glyn Dŵr. The fight was on, and for the first decade of the 15th century he led a rebellion which spread like a forest fire and in the first five years achieved incredible success. The local causes are clear, but it must also be seen as symptomatic of convulsions which wracked much of Western Europe at that time.

Owain Glyn Dŵr

The Glyn Dŵr story is among the most dramatic in British history. Although his support was recruited largely from a discontented peasantry, Owain himself was a marcher lord, a descendant of the princes of Powys and linked by blood to the family of the Llywelyns. He was also a member of the family of Ednyfed Fychan, had ties with a number of other marcher lords, and was married to a daughter of the Hanmers of Flintshire, and there were English connections and links with the royal family. Nevertheless, Owain was hailed in 1400–01 as the (self-styled) Prince of Wales. He became the spearhead of a civil war which, within the next five years, involved all Wales and the eastern Marchland, arousing echoes in many Englishmen's hearts on account of widespread disapproval of Henry IV's policies. Glyn Dŵr became the catalyst for discontent which extended far beyond the confines of Gwynedd, though it was there that he raised his earliest and most lasting support. The Tripartite Indenture of 1405 marked the height of his career. It embodied his soaring ambitions, proposing to divide the whole of South Britain into three provinces. He would be the supremo and also act directly, as Prince of Wales, over Wales and the Borderland shires. The rest of England would be divided between Percy of Northumberland administering the North and north Midlands, and Mortimer of Wigmore who would take responsibility for all England to the south. He had further plans for the Church and the

*Ruins of Ynys Seiriol
church tower*

universities. Owain conducted his 'parliaments' at three places in Merioneth—Harlech, Pennal, near Machynlleth, and Dolgellau, where his parliament house still survives. On a wave of national euphoria he was hailed as a hero, as a reincarnated Arthur.

But by 1406-7, support was falling away in Anglesey, in South Wales, and even in mid-Wales around his own estate of Sycharth. By 1409, areas affording active help were largely restricted to Caernarvonshire, Merioneth, northern Cardiganshire, and some nearby upland districts where loyalties had always been strong. The reason for disenchantment lay far and wide across Wales in the appalling devastation which had been wrought in the early years of the rebellion. Houses were destroyed, land laid waste, and churches in ruins over huge areas, and this after some fifty or more years of sickness and death during the great Plague which had reduced population and resources. No part of Wales had suffered more than Gwynedd from both the Black Death and the Rebellion, and it was in a sorrier state than had been known for centuries. Glyn Dŵr fled, an exile from justice, and none knows when and where he ended his days.

It was soon to be clear everywhere that the old order was breaking down, and during the 15th century the changing climate of thought and attitude became increasingly evident in Gwynedd. Despite the Lancastrian strictures more and more Welsh made alliances with families in the Marches and beyond. More and more went to England to be educated and to train for the law. More sought office, court favours, and became aware of the profits to be gained from trade and commerce, but without doubt the barriers were being pushed down from both sides. It was, however, the rivalries between the Houses of Lancaster and York, giving rise to the Wars of the Roses during the later years of Henry VI's reign, which were to initiate a long series of events of fateful importance for both England and Wales.

On the death of Henry VI, a dream which had hovered vaguely on the distant horizon, came into sharp focus: the main claimant to the throne on the Lancastrian side was Henry Tudor! Once more Gwynedd was central to matters of national import, for the Tudors sprang from the family of Ednyfed Fychan, distinguished seneschal of Llywelyn the Great and David, and Ednyfed's son had in turn been seneschal to Llywelyn ap Gruffydd. During the Edwardian Settlement the family had become prosperous. By the mid-14th century they were great landowners, their estates including Penmynydd in southern Anglesey. Some of them lie entombed to this day in its small church, the doors of which open to the majestic views of the Snowdonian peaks rising above the waters of Menai. At this crucial time Tudur ap Goronwy was lord of Penmynydd, and his sons through their mother were cousins

*Plas Penmynydd,
Anglesey, home of the
Tudors*

72

of Glyn Dŵr. The third of these sons was Maredudd ap Tudur, and his son Owain called himself not simply Owain ap Maredudd, but Owain ap Maredudd ap Tudur. Owain's story is well known. He became a page at the court of Henry V, and after the king's death courted and won the hand of the widowed Queen Catherine de Valois, and their sons took the surname of Tudor. In due course their elder son, Edmund, married Margaret Beaufort, daughter of the earl of Somerset, and it was through her that their son, Henry Tudor, was the main Lancastrian claimant to the throne of England. He was also, of course, grandson of ex-Queen Catherine. When Edward IV came to the throne, Henry was a child of four. He was to spend long years in Lancastrian castles in Wales, including Harlech, and later in France under the guardianship of his uncle Jasper.

*Aberconwy House,
Conway. 14th century*

*Heraldic emblems in the
Banqueting Hall of
Plas Mawr, Conway*

It was 1485 when Henry's advisers deemed the time ripe to force the issue of the Lancastrian cause. And so on 7 August he landed at Dale on Milford Haven, and with a small but determined army they marched north along the Cardigan Bay coast. At Machynlleth they were joined by more supporters from Gwynedd. So far they had been passing through Lancastrian country but, turning inland along the Dyfi, they had to strike across Yorkist Powys to reach Shrewsbury and thence moved *via* Stafford and Lichfield into Leicestershire to the small market town of Market Bosworth. There on 22 August they met Richard III's supporters, and the last battle of the Wars of the Roses was joined on Bosworth Field. Henry led his forces under the Red Dragon standard of Cadwaladr against troops who, it has been said, were too ashamed of their leader to put up the fight that might perhaps have led to victory. Whether that was so or not, Richard there met his death. The day was Henry's, and the Lancastrian cause had triumphed.

Red Dragon of Henry VIII

For Wales it had a dual significance, for a Welshman was on the throne of England, a dream fulfilled. Henry VII was fully aware of all that his countrymen hoped for, but his 24-year reign was occupied with restoring to his realm the peace and order which 29 years of war had left rudderless and chaotic. His faithful Welsh supporters were rewarded. More Welshmen appeared at court and were appointed to office. By that time many Welshmen had profited from the experience of administration in their own country, and Henry had wise and dependable advisers such as the Meyricks of Bodorgan and the Griffiths of Penrhyn, both families of Gwynedd, and many others from further afield in Wales. He lifted some of the severest burdens from his fellow countrymen, for example, the penal laws, and he suppressed lawlessness. More Welshmen studied law, while others filled the ordinary run of judicial appointments such as stewards, bailiffs,

Tudor Rose

Lion Rampant

Fleur de Lys

coroners; and eventually Welsh were able to become justices of the peace. The most valued of the new freedoms bestowed was the right of denizenship in the boroughs. But it was not without price that Henry VII made some of these concessions. The 1504 Charter of Liberties awarded to Gwynedd cost £2,000; that of 1507 a further £300. The real value of his reign was that he was able to go so far towards putting two newly-linked countries, both disenchanted and disorientated after long years of war and civil unrest, back on the road to peace. The authority of the Crown was now accepted throughout England and Wales, and the slow but steady progress which more than twenty years of Tudor reign had brought, pointed the way forward. But many of the changes moved to the detriment of traditional Welsh life and institutions, and increasing destruction of things Welsh was an unhappy outcome.

By the time Henry VIII came to the throne in 1509, much had still to be accomplished. The most significant political event for Wales was the passing in 1536 of the Act of Union of England and Wales. It was not so much a new move as the natural culmination of Tudor policy that had swung to the English viewpoint more and more since the battle of Bosworth. To bring the two countries not only into full union, but also politically in line, the marcher lordships were abolished, and in their place eight new counties were created to complete the 13 shires of Wales and Monmouth as they remained until 1974. Gwynedd, of course, was shired already by 1284. The 1542 Act which followed was virtually an extension of the earlier Act of Union, but two innovations were: first, the establishment of the Court of Great Sessions in Wales and making it independent of Westminster, and second the representation for the first time of each of the Welsh shires and Cheshire in parliament. Independently of these political reforms, Henry VIII was building up both a navy and the two countries' coastal defences. The two early Tudors had prepared a platform on which Modern Wales could begin to build. It is with aspects of the later development of Gwynedd on these historical foundations that the rest of this volume is concerned.

Elizabethan silver chalice and paten cover

XII Land and the People

Change is less immediately evident in the rural landscape of Gwynedd than might be expected after centuries of eventful history: indeed, on vast areas of its more barren and more remote countryside the fingers of Time have pressed with exceeding lightness. Under the tribal régime of the Middle Ages agrarian progress was virtually unknown. Partible inheritance brought about the morcellation of holdings, and within the clans the status of bond and free was the rigid foundation of the social pattern. It was only under the Tudors that the tide of change crept gently in. Medieval conditions of tenure then gave place at an increasing pace to new concepts of landholding, and had profound effects on both the land and the people. The amassing of land into personal estates was not new, but both process and results accelerated during the 16th century. By the 17th century great estates were practising commercial agriculture and playing a dominant rôle in the economy of the country. The new class of the gentry became central figures in rural society and were to remain so during the 18th and much of the 19th centuries. Bond status ceased to exist, and bond and free gave place to gentry, a middle class (difficult to define, but real), the peasantry, and alas! the destitute. Visible evidence of change included the revision of field boundaries, the introduction of dry-stone walling, and hedges; the enclosing of parkland; great houses (*plasau*) which were rebuilt or erected and added to as wealth and fashion urged; and the reclamation from the 18th century onwards of commons and marsh.

John Jones, a Roundhead of Merioneth, executed 1660

   Strongly contrasted landscapes within the three counties brought different responses, but in most parts remoteness from English influences and their late impact, even compared with many other parts of Wales, were universally felt. In the lower and more fertile districts agriculture progressed more rapidly, notably in Anglesey's higher production of corn, and this despite extensive 'bosslands', where old hard rocks protrude through a thin soil, and natural marsh long precluded the development of the Malltraeth depression. In the vast mountain core of Caernarvonshire and Merioneth, sheer altitude and paucity of soil cover have ever defeated Man's efforts to farm it for any length of time except as upland grazing. It is the richer vales and coastlands, large stretches of their surface deep in glacial drift, or in riverine and marine silts, which provide the best farmland, suitable

PRINCIPATVS WALLIÆ PARS BOREALIS Vulgo NORTH WALES

for either crops or beasts, and their value is enhanced further by the mild marine climate and only offset by distance from major markets, except in periods of nationwide difficulty. These last include economic depression, hostilities, such as the Civil and the Napoleonic Wars, and years of poor harvests. Physical factors and remoteness combined with inadequate communications operate particularly against Merioneth.

Population figures reflect the relative position of the three counties over four centuries. Percentages prior to the first official Census of 1801 are necessarily based on estimates, but the concurrence of a number of authorities gives them a measure of reliability.

Borwnnog Grammar School, founded 1618

COUNTY TOTALS EXPRESSED AS PERCENTAGES OF THEIR 1971 POPULATION

	Mid–16th century	1670	1801	1901	Total 1971	Date of peak population
	%	%	%	%		
Anglesey	18	27	56	85	56,761	1971
Caernarvonshire ..	12	21	34	96	123,064	1921
Merioneth	30	55	83	139	33,330	1881

The change in numbers of dwellings by no means follows the population curve, for family size peaked in the Victorian era, especially in the towns, dropping dramatically toward the 1970s. Nevertheless, abandoned cottages are far from rare in the poorer districts, and on the former commons, but the general picture has altered less than population numbers as regards habitations. The most startling feature of the Table is the decline in Merioneth's population from the 1880s. This progressive century-long decrease first became evident in 1881 Census figures, a trend shared with Radnorshire, a county with comparable problems. It was due in part to heavy emigration overseas, to the flight from the land following enclosures of the commons, and the resulting search for work in the rising industrial towns of South Wales, the Midlands, and the London area. But towns as well as rural districts suffered population losses in Merioneth. Anglesey's growth curve levelled out from 1861, but after a period of minor fluctuations, began a steady rise which has been maintained since World War II. Caernarvonshire's population changes have not been dissimilar, though its rate of growth was maintained until the beginning of the present century, then slowed to decline, and was resumed after World War I.

The accession of the Tudors, hailed as deliverers by the Welsh, and followed by the Act of Union, tumbled the last barriers to progress. A new mood ensued, and the growing numbers of Welsh who were educated at English schools and universities, or who had qualified

*Plas Penmynydd,
home of the Tudors*

in the Law at the Inns of Court, acted as further leaven. Thenceforward, more of their countrymen sought to follow the English lead in many economic, commercial, and educational fields. The first grammar schools were founded: Friars' School, Bangor (1557); Llanrwst School, founded by Sir Richard Wynn (1565); and Botwnnog Grammar School in Llŷn (1618). Further, the taste for urban life was growing, although it had never previously been characteristic of Wales, and within the towns the social and economic barriers were slowly collapsing, while in the countryside the medieval order was also crumbling.

The main change in rural society was the rise of the gentry. They had varied origins. In Anglesey, Hwfa ap Cynddelw was one of the three clan chiefs of ancient Anglesey stock whose descendants are traceable as landowners in Malltraeth and the northern commotes from the 15th century onwards. But the Meyricks of Bodorgan and the Griffiths of Llanedwen, both of the Penrhyn stock, came from the mainland, and the Griffiths were among a number of Welsh of ancient lineage whom the Tudors brought into prominence. Their later fate varied: for example, Clenennau, its great house the centre of a large estate for 400 years, became a farm. A number of important families from England built up large holdings. Among these were the Bulkeleys of Cheadle, Cheshire, who had settled in Anglesey before the Battle of Bosworth, accumulating property there and in Caernarvonshire, to become one of the wealthiest and most influential families in Wales, and building the mansion of Baron Hill, near Beaumaris. Much later, Sir John Stanley, a connection of the Stanleys of Lancashire and Cheshire, acquired the Penrhos estate on Holy Island through his marriage. The Vaughans of Nannau and Hengwrt in Merioneth are descended from a cousin of Owain Glyn Dŵr. The story is that this cousin, Howel Sele, was entertaining Owain, when in a quarrel in the surrounding woods Howel attacked Owain, but was himself killed, and his body, so presumed, was only found years afterwards hidden in a tree trunk. The great house which he visited is there no longer, and the newer mansion, Nannau, has replaced it. In the same county many became involved in the commercial development of their estates, increasing their acreages by various means, and some later estate holders have actually climbed to the status of gentry as a result of their success in trade and commerce, for example, through the woollen industry of Merioneth.

Collections of family papers throw considerable light on the rural history of Gwynedd during these centuries. From the 15th century onwards the Bulkeley documents include records of sales, leases, and grants by which the extension of their estate can be traced. Scattered strips in common fields were compacted, portions of commons enclosed, and turbaries, meadows, and tenements purchased or otherwise come by. From initial holdings in Llanfaes and Beaumaris, their property spread eventually into every one of Anglesey's six commotes as well as into Caernarvonshire. On a rather more modest scale the Meyricks of Bodorgan also purchased, exchanged, and enclosed more acreage. A number of landowners still continued to insist on medieval dues and renders and on the services which had been obligatory in the Middle Ages, but gradually they died out, and the part played by the gentry in modernising agriculture and promoting commerce became of prime importance. Herds and crops increased and as the corn harvests became more bountiful, more mills were erected on Bulkeley and Meyrick lands and on other estates, both the windmills and the water-mills once so widespread and characteristic a feature of the Anglesey scene. The Bulkeleys also employed numbers of estate workers and domestic servants, ran a tannery in Beaumaris, and owned a lime kiln and no fewer than 20 quarries 'on Sir Richard's freehold wastes' in Anglesey.

The lovely sheltered and fertile vale of Conwy and the nearby Creuddyn peninsula were the sites of a number of flourishing estates in the 17th century. The Bulkeleys of Baron Hill held Maenan, a large disparate property extending from Llanfairfechan to the Great Orme and southward into Nant Conwy. Farming there brought in £500 per annum and rents almost £3,400, much of their wealth also originated in the timber trade, and in addition the wood supplied many needs, such as fencing and building on their own estates. Another considerable property was held at Caerhun by the Davieses, and near Llanrwst the Wynns held Gwydir, the largest of the Conwy valley estates. Descended from Owain Gwynedd, they built their mansion, Gwydir Castle, on the site of a 7th-century fort and a 14th-century watch tower. Numerous additions had been made to the house before it fell into ruins in the present century, since when it has been restored and

Plas Mawr, Conway

refurnished by a former bank manager. The best-known of the Wynns was Sir John, who developed the estate on commercial lines in the 17th century and is said to have employed at least eight agents and stewards and farmed four times the acreage of Maenan. His major crop, too, was timber, felled from the great stands on nearby hillsides and in the Lledr valley. The policy of timber exploitation was continued by his son-in-law who maintained the estate largely by selling timber, principally oak, and processed by his own sawyers and coopers for export through the port of Caernarvon whence it was shipped to Liverpool.

The style of living of the wealthier landowners varied, some maintaining large houses luxuriously equipped, others preferring medium-sized establishments comfortable, but traditional in furbishing.

*Sir John Owen
of Clenennau*

Gwydir was splendid enough for the entertainment of royalty; Baron Hill newer with lavish furnishings and surrounded, as was Gwydir, with large gardens and a park. The Morgans of Henblas and the William Bulkeleys of Brynddu (both Anglesey) had more modest accommodation and their furniture and equipment were comparatively sparse, the hall of the latter paved with stone flags and vary bare. In most Welsh homes at this time the furniture was solid and plain, but linen was in ample supply. The houses of the middle and lesser rank gentry typically consisted of a passage hall, the full height of the building, a parlour or two, kitchen, dairy, and brewhouse, with quite commodious bedrooms above and outbuildings nearby. The 18th century saw the introduction of widespread improvements: more tasteful furnishings, better clothes and style of living, and the rebuilding or extension of many residences of the gentry. By that time, there were many Anglo-Welsh marriages, and family and other English connections meant that fashions were no longer delayed in reaching Welsh society.

The emergence of a middle class was associated principally with the increase in commercial activities and the numbers following a profession. They were therefore to be found mainly, though not exclusively, in the towns. Merchants, clergy, lawyers, army and naval officers, together with freemen who had become successful farmers, contributed the greater number in this group. But those successful in trade, from drovers to shopkeepers, became sufficiently prosperous to educate their children and many of these, too, rose in the social scale. In her study of *Social Life in Mid-Eighteenth Century Anglesey* G. Nesta Evans selected the home of Lewis Morris as probably typical of his class. One of the Morris Brothers, whose letters, maps, and charts are of such value in relation to the period, lived in solid comfort, keeping a very good table, and the house consisted of a study, parlour, kitchen, and bedrooms. Lady Evans mentions its sash windows as representative of what was then middle-class luxury.

The third class was typified by the lesser farmers and smallholders, by upper domestic servants, and local craftsmen, such as carpenters, shoemakers, thatchers and stonemasons. Few of them had substantial incomes, and most of them lived in simple stone-built cottages with two or at most three small rooms, some with a byre or workshop attached. Fish and potatoes were usually in ample supply, but the poorest lived mainly on stews, 'porridges', oaten cakes, barley or rye bread, and such wild fruits, birds, fish, and animals as could be secured from time to time. This was the group, domestic servants apart, which was most easily reduced to poverty when epidemics or famine struck, and who at such periods were liable to die or become destitute.

A Telford mile stone on the
lyhead Road (A5).

33. Menai Bridge. A text book example of bridgehead growth. Formerly
Porthaethwy, a ferry terminus, its modern development dates from 1826.

(*right*) Holyhead: a toll house dating from the building
the Telford road.

(*below*) Telford's Menai Bridge, built 1826.

36. The damming of the river Cefni, Anglesey, which drains the Malltraeth depression.

37. Bodedern, Anglesey, an early woollen mill.

38. St Cybi's complex, Llangybi.

39. Farmland at Llangaffo, Anglesey.

40. An early picture of Porthmadog Harbour.

41. Threshing at Star Farm, Gaerwen, Anglesey, around 1900.

For the better part of two hundred years after Union, farming in more distant parts of Wales was shackled by traditional methods, a limited range of crops, and backward communications. Sleds were commoner on the farm than wheeled vehicles, and, except for the share and coulter, ploughs long continued to be made of wood, operated by hand, in some cases drawn by oxen, and more rarely by horses. In addition, the smaller farmer used such implements as the flail, the hay hook, and the peat cutter, adding to his own hard labour. During and after the late 18th century, the range of crops was slowly widened as new agrarian ideas filtered in from England, and especially from Norfolk. Edward Wynne is credited with introducing the Norfolk four-course rotation into Merioneth, and the not very popular turnip in particular. It was said to be scorned as an uneatable vegetable, even poison, and thrown to the dogs. In due course its value was realised as part of a succession of root crops (mainly turnips and potatoes) in the

18th-century Welsh harp

seasons between corn and re-seeded grass. The last two replaced the soil nutriment which the corn had taken from it, and the grass involved turning in the sward by deeper ploughing.

But soils were poor over vast stretches of Gwynedd—shallow, thin, and acid, except over limestone and where glacial soils and recent silts overlie the bedrock. Manuring had long relied on dung, or, on the coasts, on seaweed, but during the 18th century not only crop rotation but the value of lime came to be recognised as a fertiliser. Anglesey had been using its local limestone for this purpose, as well as importing it from as early as 1666. Now importation of lime, much of it from South Wales, took place through the many small ports around the coasts of Caernarvonshire and Merioneth also, the lime burnt in the kilns on the shore, their ruins still sometimes traceable. The estates had been using nitrogenous crops to renew the soil from the second decade of the 18th century, and in addition to cultivating roots as a field crop were planting orchards and creating gardens. Edward Corbet of Ynysmaengwyn in Merioneth was one of the pioneers in the south of Gwynedd, together with William Oakley of Tan y bwlch.

These and others were also turning their attention increasingly to the improvement of animal breeds. Cattle trading dominated the upland economy, increasing in the 16th century, and reaching a peak in the 17th century. It was only later that sheep achieved a more important place in mountain districts which had earlier specialised in cattle, and raised in addition pathetically thin crops of barley, oats, and perhaps a few vegetables. The 17th-century picture was very different from the familiar one of today. Then the drovers became the most successful traders in Wales, and their 'roads', which were mere cattle tracks for the most part, netted the entire country in series of west-east lines linked by subsidiaries. For some three hundred years their cattle were driven on the hoof into local Welsh markets and fairs, but the growth of the far wider trade into Borderland, Midland, and even London markets became of far greater profitability. The small native Welsh Black breed was at first predominant, though eventually supplemented by animals of larger carcass. In Gwynedd, however, then as now, Welsh Blacks were preferred for poorer pastures. A number of estate owners were 'drovers', but most were farmers, merchants, and organisers, who had turned to this lucrative side of cattle raising. A number became their own bankers, some issuing their own bank notes. Their status in society rose with their wealth. So did their style of life, and both the men and their womenfolk became leaders of fashions in dress. They bought more land and built good houses. They took part in local politics, travelled widely, bringing back seeds and cuttings which widened the range of crops and trees on their land and were then taken up and introduced by others.

Their success altered the balance within pastoral farming, bringing about a reduction in the number of milch cows kept, and those mainly for breeding, and to supply the household with dairy products. Even more significant in relation to today, the age-old custom of trans-humance gradually died out, not only due to the drovers, but also to the later enclosures of the upland pastures. This had involved, for centuries, the movement of herds and herdsmen to summer pastures at the *hafod* (summer dwelling) on the mountain, and the return with the butter and cheeses which were made there, to the *hendre* (meaning the old, i.e., permanent, township) in the valley each autumn when the herd was thinned to compensate for the paucity of winter pasture. The practice persisted in Gwynedd until the last quarter of the 18th century when, with the successful introduction of root crops, winter fodder became available. Traces of the *hafodau* may still be found, in place-names such as *hafod* and *hendre*. The drovers, too, have left their mark in the names of inns, and in the drovers' tracks themselves. The actual droving was usually done by the drover's cattle-men, who covered a few miles a day with their herds over the long rough 'roads' which were in most parts little more than hill tracks. At night the cattle were herded into reserved fields along the route, and the men either slept rough or in barns or buildings behind the inns. Since their day a lot of the inns have changed their names, but some survive, and widespread over England and Wales can still be seen names such as *The Drovers' Arms* and *The Black Ox*.

In addition to cattle, numbers of sheep and goats were kept for their milk, and goat's flesh was eaten as well as mutton, but the impor- tance of sheep-raising for their wool began to supersede the droving

The Ship Inn, Aberdaron

82

trade and only then did sheep largely replace cattle in the mountain economy. South Welsh wool and woollen cloth had been featuring at English fairs from the 14th century. By 1500 the Welsh cloth industry had moved northward, and Denbighshire and Merioneth had become established as cloth-producing centres, their trade expanding markedly after Union. Until the 16th century, Shrewsbury maintained a stranglehold on sales of wool and cloth, but later the market widened, prosperity increased in the country as a whole, and the Welsh industry benefited. Manufacture alone remained rural, operating in cottages and farmhouses and in some small country towns. For a long time Merioneth was Gwynedd's main producer of woollens, output centring on the districts around Dolgellau and Bala.

In the late 18th century when, in country districts, all food and clothing were produced on the farm, every farmhouse and cottage was involved in some type of woollen production, be it spinning, weaving, or knitting. A carding bench, a spinning wheel, or a hand loom would be found in the kitchen or in a lean-to loom shed, and by these products the family income was supplemented prior to the factory period. Women and children alike were concerned, and it was said

A spinster

that some of the children could knit before they could talk! In some of the eastern border valleys of Merioneth they would arrange social 'knitting nights' in each others' homes and *'y noswaith neu'* would be enlivened by singing or by one of the menfolk playing the *crwth* or the harp, or reciting if they deigned to be present. The output of this domestic woollen industry was considerable. Bala sent out remarkably large quantities of web cloth, stockings, and gloves, yielding an estimated annual profit of £53,000 during the 1770s. In lesser quantities Anglesey made a blue cloth, Caernarvonshire a drab greyish-brown one. In 1642 an Act of Parliament lifted trading restrictions from Welsh 'cottons' (coatings), thus freeing them to enter over 200 fairs and markets in Wales and the Borderland, and still more were exported through Barmouth and Bristol. The Caernarvonshire industry was long in the hands of cottage workers, only fulling being carried out in the widespread *pandai* (fulling mills) until the 19th century when the first weaving mills were opened. With the expansion of the industry, many local fairs and markets benefited—not only older centres such as Dolgellau and Bala, but lesser ones such as Aberffraw and Llanerchymedd in Anglesey. So, too, did the market and port of Caernarvon. The cloth industry spread as other places built carding mills, and, later, weaving mills. Early examples were Dolgarrog, Bodedern, Penmachno, Llanwnda, Llanrug, and, soon after it was founded, Tremadoc. Cloth-making proved particularly well adapted to Gwynedd's economy, and it is still widespread as a rural and small town industry in the three counties.

XIII The North Wales Coast Route in the Pre-Railway Era

Whether in war or peace the most important route in North Wales is without question that which follows the northern coastal shelf and, crossing Anglesey, links Holyhead with Chester. Its value to Gwynedd lies not only in the route itself, but because from it diverge north-south roads along the west coast of Wales, through the valleys of Snowdonia, and the Vale of Conwy. The section from Chester to the Conwy presents few problems apart from the hazards of weather and high tides, but from the point where it reaches the eastern bank of the Conwy estuary, both the coast road and its southern feeders are or may be beset by difficulties, some seasonal, some at all times. Only when the comparatively level stretches across Anglesey were reached could even the most intrepid traveller prior to Telford's day feel his sense of insecurity fall away.

Both the Conwy estuary and the Menai Straits offered major obstacles to the traveller by land, but the shallow waters of Beddmanarch Bay which separate Holy Island from the main island of Anglesey seem not to have been difficult to cross, either to Penrhos, where Telford later built the Stanley Embankment, or at Pont rhyd y bont, the narrowest point and later the site of Four Mile Bridge. From prehistoric times to the present day, the old harbour of Caergybi or the newer harbours of its successor Holyhead were the landing point for much traffic across the Irish Sea, especially from Dublin.

From the Middle Ages and later there is ample information concerning the Conwy and Menai ferries. Giraldus Cambrensis described the boats used as made of twigs, almost round, and covered inside and out with raw hide, not dissimilar from the type of coracle to be seen on Welsh rivers until recent times, and even to the present day on some. By the 17th and 18th centuries the ferry boats were much bigger, but little safer when laden with passengers and frightened horses. There were ferries higher up the Conwy at Tal y cafn and at Llanrwst before the bridge was built (which so long remained the lowest bridging point on the river), but these ferries and the bridge involved a long détour if they were used by travellers from Chester. Anglesey was served in the Middle Ages by no fewer than seven ferries, operating from Llanfaes, Beaumaris, Porthaethwy (now the site of Menai Bridge), Llanidan, and Abermenai on the Anglesey side, and from Porthesgob (Garth) and Caernarvon on the southern shore. Llanfaes ferry in the

Old Llanrwst bridge over the River Conwy

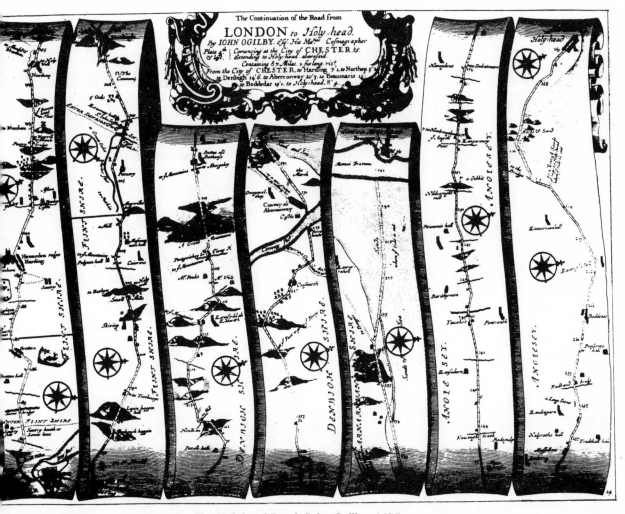

Map 10. The Holyhead Road, John Ogilby, 1675.

time of the princes served the court and royal manor of the commote of Dindaethwy prior to the evacuation of the people of Llanfaes to Newborough. After the new town was planned in 1302, Beaumaris took over the Llanfaes ferry traffic, and Abermenai served the new settlement. Ferrying rights were very valuable on a major route such as this. That at Porthesgob, later known as the Bangor ferry, belonged to the bishops of Bangor as its name implies, and in 1721 it was described (as was Porthaethwy) as being 'on the great road from London to Holyhead'. There is also a tradition that Archbishop Baldwin during his mammoth journey around Wales in 1188 preached the Crusade on the rocks at Porthaethwy. It is thought that the bishop's

85

fairs in Bangor may have extended to Porthaethwy, for it had 'a passage of beasts' as early as 1407-9, and four fairs a year in 1691.

With the upturn in the economy in Tudor times and increasing production and trade, the ports reflected it. Caernarvon, Beaumaris, and Chester were trading in dairy produce, wool, hides and leather as a result of expansion in animal farming. In the Middle Ages, Chester had become the head port of North Wales, and so of the subsidiary ports on its coasts, and from Chester there continued to be dispatched English and foreign goods for redistribution to the markets and fairs of Anglesey and Caernarvonshire. The expanding trade through the ports was paralleled by that in their small markets and fairs. Slate and fish gained in importance both in local markets and in exports, increasing notably in the 17th and 18th centuries, not only at Caernarvon and Conway, but at the bishop's fairs at Bangor and Garth. Thus, slowly but steadily, traffic on the roads multiplied, and this was the case not only locally but in long-distance movement, particularly from London to Ireland. During the reign of Elizabeth I the Irish Mail began to carry 'the Queen's packets' to that country, and in 1599 Holyhead was designated a permanent posting station for the royal posts, some of which had previously gone through Chester. The London-Holyhead road then ran through St Albans, Coventry, Nantwich, Chester, Rhuddlan, and Beaumaris, except for the years 1572-5, when the mails passed through Liverpool instead of North Wales, reverting to the Holyhead route in 1575. There was not infrequent alteration in the post stations for a time, but, in 1599, a permanent line was established by Order in Council with posts at Chester (then known as West Chester), Rhuddlan, Conway, Beaumaris, and Holyhead. Northop was added in 1602, and Llangefni in 1626. There was a postmaster appointed at each, typically a local innkeeper, the inn doubling to act as a post office and to serve travellers. The ferry points varied from time to time. In 1608 Robert Lloyd's *Survey* showed them at Abermenai, Moel y don, and Porthaethwy. At the end of the 17th century, with traffic building up from a widening area, another route was being followed increasingly. This was shown on Robert Norden's map of North Wales, published in 1694, as linking the West Midlands with Caernarvon *via* Welshpool, Dollgellau, Harlech, and Dolbenmaen, and prior to this in 1675 in John Ogilby's *Britannia*, a short cut in the direct route was marked between Porthaethwy and Holyhead. This section of the road was to be of increasing importance from that time onwards. Ogilby's 1720 edition also depicted a road from Abermenai to near Newborough, thence to Llangaffo, Aberffraw, and Llanfaelog, though extending no further than Llanfair yn Neubwll. However, with Beaumaris as the shire town of Anglesey and supporting

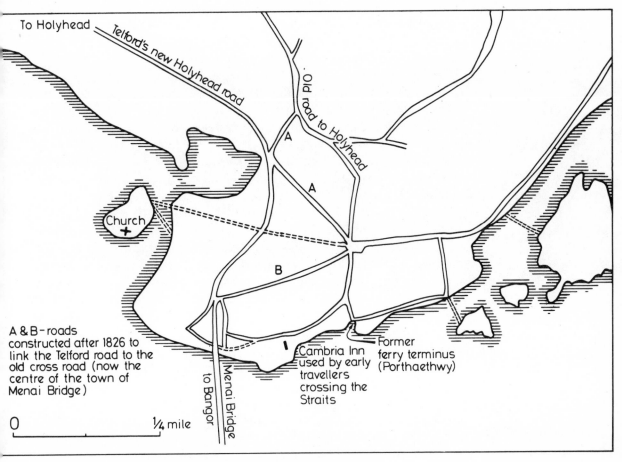

Map 11. Menai Bridge District: Roads, 1843.

two weekly markets, and Holyhead, although small and scattered, nevertheless commanding the shortest crossing to the mid-east coast of Ireland, it was between these two places that most traffic moved across the island, apart from that from Bangor to Holyhead. A major step forward was the turnpiking of the Porthaethwy to Holyhead road in 1765. It was widened, and tolls were levied by 1808 at four gates. The journey was made more comfortable by hostelries, and Pennant travelling this way remarked on the good inns at Gwindy and Bangor, while at Holyhead there was the famous *Eagle and Child,* as well as two others.

But on the mainland matters were less propitious. The road from Degannwy to Bangor continued dangerous, and travellers faced every prospect of delay. Storms could whip the Conwy estuary to fury, and at low tide the sandbanks continually shifted. The ferrymen were both dilatory and rapacious, and although the 17th-century ferry boats were big enough to carry both passengers and horses, there is a record of one sinking during the Commonwealth with the loss of all but one of its 80 passengers. Immediately after leaving Conway, Penmaenbach drops in a sheer precipice to the seashore, and except at low neaps the sands could not be negotiated by coaches. Consequently the alternative, but still steep and hazardous, Sychnant Pass was used by them, and by all other vehicles until Penmaenbach was eventually tunnelled in 1931–5. The precipitous north face of Penmaenmawr some three miles further along the road was almost as intractable a problem, although in 1686 Lord Clarendon's coach was manhandled *across* the mountain 'by three brave and stalwart fellows'! In 1720, a new road was cut, seven feet wide, on the seaward side of Penmaenmawr, but travellers could be bombarded by falling rocks from above, storms might lash the seaward edge, and rock falls break the road sides. In 1769, parliament at last decided that a new road should be built nearer the foot of the mountain. It was the third road to be constructed round the headland. Built by John Sylvester as engineer, it was protected by a wall on either side, and Dr. Johnson after travelling this way in 1774 described it as 'very easy and very safe'. Traces of it may still be seen.

For a very long time the Lavan sands were crossed by riders and coaches, setting off usually from Aber and reaching Beaumaris at the Anglesey side. Drovers also swam their cattle across the narrow ribbon of water which remained at low tide. Coaches crossed only if the water was sufficiently shallow, otherwise passengers were conveyed by ferry boat, repeating the delays and risks which bedevilled the Conwy ferry. There are stories of ferrymen so drunk in the Beaumaris inns that nothing would persuade them to their boats, and when luckless travellers were in danger of being drowned by the rising tide they were forced to leave their baggage and swim across.

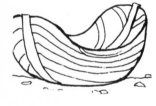

*17th-century Beaumaris
ferry boat*

Early wayfarers went perforce on foot or on horseback. The postboys rode, carrying the mail this way probably from the time of Elizabeth I, and certainly from 1635 when Charles I appointed one Thomas Witherings His Majesty's Postmaster, and made all mail, private or official, a government monopoly. The postboys were equipped with leather bags for the mail, and a horn which they had to sound four times in every mile. Coaches date back to the time of Elizabeth I, but it is unlikely that any were seen on Welsh roads unless they were owned by the wealthy, probably the nobility. The 17th century was the great coach-building period, by which time the main highways were very slowly being improved following the 1555 *Highway Act* which took away the responsibility for road maintenance from the parishes. But the real improvements began with the Turnpike Trusts. In England they date from 1663, but Wales lagged behind, especially in the poorer and more remote mountainous districts. As coach building and road construction exerted their mutual influence, the public stage coach had come into being, and the first known to run to timetable plied between Birmingham and Chester in 1637, travelling *via* Nantwich. Twenty years later a regular service ran three times a week between London and Chester, but it was not until 1776 that this service was extended to Holyhead. Meantime there came into being, as a result of a scheme proposed by the 7th Viscount Bulkeley, a carriage road through the Sychnant Pass from Conway and down to the coast again on the east side of Penmaenmawr. By 1776, a regular coach service used this road, followed in 1785 by the Royal Mails. The mails then ran twice weekly on the post road through Conway, Beaumaris, Penmynydd, across the river Ceint, to Llangefni, Bode-dern, Pont rhyd y bont (Four Mile Bridge) and so to Holyhead. It is still known as the post road. In 1765, the first *Turnpike Act* for Anglesey provided for the widening of the road from Porthaethwy to Holyhead and for the levying of tolls at new turnpikes. In 1718 Beaumaris became a sub-office, Bangor the main one, and this resulted in the switching of the post road from Beaumaris to the Bangor-Porthaethwy crossing of the Straits, the new post road joining the old one at Ceint. Apart from the new Sychnant road, Caernarvonshire by this time was lagging badly behind and had some of the worst roads in North Wales until, spurred on it would seem by the landlord of the *White Lion* at Chester, the first Caernarvonshire *Turnpike Act* was passed in 1769. The road came to be known as the Old Caernarvonshire Turnpike, and ran from Conway to the Bangor ferry, then on to Caernarvon and Pwllheli.

A stretch of the Penmaenmawr coast road

The late 18th century had already witnessed profound stirrings of economic life and of land development in rural Wales. Population was increasing slowly but steadily, markets growing, and the ports registering large numbers of vessels and mounting cargoes. Caernarvon, for example, had almost 250 vessels concerned with the shipping of slate by that time, and nearly 2,000 coasting vessels and 1,000 foreign ships cleared the port. It was therefore not surprising that, when in 1783 plans were put forward for a bridge across the Straits, they were opposed by Caernarvon. And nothing was done. But in 1800 the Bill was passed for the Union of Ireland with Great Britain. The situation was changed. Not only was fast contact with Ireland imperative as never before, but mails were multiplying and passenger traffic mounting. In 1780, Robert Lawrence, a Shrewsbury innkeeper, anxious to divert the lucrative North Welsh traffic from the Chester route, secured the support of a group of London inkeepers and promoted the first stage coach which travelled from the capital to the North Wales coast *via* Shrewsbury, Llangollen, Corwen, and Llanrwst to Conway. In the latter half of the 18th century an increasing number of roads were turnpiked across the width of North Wales, and Lord Penrhyn, active in the development of slate quarries in the Bethesda area, had built a new road through the Nant Ffrancon. By 1800 this road had been extended to Capel Curig, where he had built an inn to accommodate 60 travellers. The actual route of this road in the vale was later superseded, but it was Lord Penrhyn's initiative which was instrumental in first opening up the northern end of a new approach road to the coast. Irish M.P.s, too, were pressing for better and faster roads. Madocks at this time was pushing the Porthdinllaen project with a view to diverting traffic from Holyhead and so favouring further the development of the Traeth Mawr area. But parliament voted by a narrow margin for the Holyhead route, and in 1808 the Royal Irish Mail was re-routed through Shrewsbury, Capel Curig, and Bangor.

In 1810, a Parliamentary Committee sat on the question of Holyhead roads and its harbour, the latter by then in pressing need of development. It was the beginning of a major step forward in the extension of the road system. Rennie drew plans for a new Conway bridge, but they were turned down, and in the following year one, Thomas Telford, submitted a report on the Shrewsbury route and another design for a bridge across the Conwy. Although the need for bridges across both the Conwy and the Straits was urgent, it was only in 1815 that Telford's plans were passed, and he got to work on the stretch of road between Cerrig y drudion and Bangor. By 1819, the journey from London to Holyhead, which so recently had taken several days, was reduced from 38 to 36 hours. In addition, coaches were running from Liverpool and Manchester *via* Chester into North Wales, and as a result three mail coaches and two stage coaches crossed Anglesey each way every day, only those through Chester now using the coast route through Conway. (The Liverpool and Manchester coach, however, only ran for 12 months.) In 1820, the building of Menai Bridge began. Telford's plans for the Conway Bridge were approved the following year, and work started on it in 1822.

Thomas Telford

This remarkable architect-engineer, 'the father of civil engineering', played a part of incalculable importance in the opening up of Gwynedd's roads. Brilliantly and beautifully designed bridges, aqueducts, buildings, roads, and canals in Shropshire and Scotland had brought him fame before he became the architect of the new Holyhead Road from Shrewsbury, including the two superb suspension bridges which, from 1826, carried it across the Conwy estuary and the

Menai Straits. Thomas Telford had achieved the miracle essential to convert this Holyhead Road and the old coast road from Chester into a major artery of economic and commercial life. The crossing of the Lavan Sands and the Conway and Menai ferries became outmoded memories, and Porthaethwy gave place to the new bridgehead town of Menai Bridge. At Holy Island's harbour, which had received Irish incomers from prehistoric traders onwards, the future of the modernised and growing port and town of Holyhead was advanced one step further. Its rôle as a railway terminus had still to develop.

Conwy Ferry
A 1795 print by Edward Pugh.

XIV   The Great Enclosures

Y Traeth Mawre, being a haven, having no habitation nor resort.
And there is likewise neither ship, vessel, or boat that belongeth
to the same.—*State Papers*, 1565.

The 19th century in Britain was a period of more rapid advances
in the economy than had been witnessed in any previous century. On
the coalfields the roots of modern industry dated back to the latter
half of the 18th century, as did improvements leading to modern
agriculture. But Gwynedd, still basically rural, continued to lag behind
England and the Borderland despite the lead given by the more
progressive estates, for the typical farmer and smallholder rarely
profited from their example before 1800. However, the ground for
advancement had been prepared by widening opportunities in
education. In addition, communications were improving and rising
prosperity resulted from trade and commerce and from such industries
as slate quarrying and the mining of metalliferous ores. As the century
advanced the slow tide of change became a flood. The population of
England and Wales increased by between three-and-a-half and four
times. By 1851, the ratio of urban to rural residents had equalised;
by 1901 it was 77:23. There could have been no greater stimulus to
commercial farming. Even in remote areas self-sufficient subsistence

*Wheels of a light
opening plough for
use with Welsh
hill pony*

farming became outward looking, and in varying degrees commer-
cialised. To achieve this, agriculture in Gwynedd had to take on a
new face. The region was most affected by the rise of large urban
markets in South Wales and the Midlands; to a lesser extent by those
of northern England and the London area. Animal farming in Gwynedd
was especially backward in matters such as breeding and the provision
of winter feed. To satisfy the growing demand for fresh meat
throughout the year, the old practices of thinning the herds in autumn
and depending on sparse supplies of salt meat during the winter had to
be abandoned. Dairy produce similarly had to be produced all the
year round, and in larger quantities. Cropping faced various problems.
Merioneth farmers were still on an oats-barley-oats-barley rotation
ad infinitum, and the soil was consequently exhausted, depending
solely on manure to restore its fertility. With the introduction of a cropping sequence such as oats, clover, wheat, turnips, winter feed became
available and the soil was replenished with nitrogen. Archaic ploughs
long survived in use, especially in the remote districts—remote not

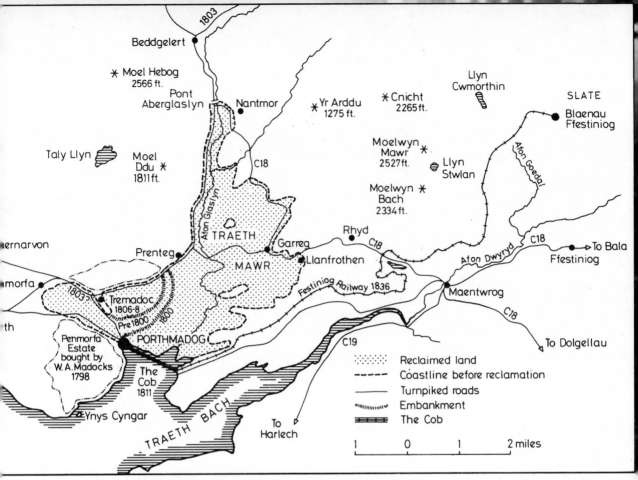

Map 12. The Reclamation of Traeth Mawr, based on Elisabeth Beazley.

only in that ideas filtered through slowly, but remote also from centres of an advancing iron industry. In Anglesey, only five per cent. of the land was under tillage in the late 18th century, yet 90,000 bushels of oats and barley were exported. There were everywhere two matters of urgency: to provide more pasture (and this meant the better use of hill slopes) and the reclamation of marshland to bring more acreage into production and so increase the vital hay crops and permanent pasture.

By the 18th century growing numbers of landless led to squatting on the commons, the building of *tai un nos* (houses constructed in one night), poor hovels with a little land also enclosed in one night. Groups of squatters formed new communities, for example in Llanfechell and Moelfre (Ang.) and Rhoshirwaun (Llŷn). During the 19th-century enclosure phases, many were evicted, some allowed to retain their holdings by payment, or granted them free if they had been resident for 20 years or more. Some *hafodau* were converted into hill farms, so short was pasture. There had been overgrazing on the commons for centuries where stock could be depastured without stint, and where

93

Old breast plough, Merioneth

there were in many cases additional rights such as free warren and turbary, the latter had resulted in areas of bare rock and serious soil loss. The Napoleonic Wars further heightened the demand for food and timber, and enclosures were effected by private Act and later by General Enclosure Acts. Wheat prices soared, encouraging the ploughing up of permanent pasture, and grazing being sought on ever poorer land. The navy's demand for timber for shipbuilding reduced Gwynedd's woodlands, compensating the loss to some extent by releasing new farmland, but ravishing areas of great beauty about which Thomas Pennant had waxed lyrical in his descriptions of magnificent groves of oak and birch in Merioneth, and especially in the Rhaiadr du district where 'Cader Idris appears in full majesty over . . . sloping forests'. Walter Davies in his *General View of Agriculture in Wales* (1810) deplored this deforestation, but noted that there had been already some replanting in Merioneth.

Many of the new landless took advantage of the developments in fishing, mining, and slate quarrying, where workmen's cottages had enough land attached to provide a vegetable patch and pasture for a milch cow, a goat or two, and room for a few domestic fowl. These dwellings may still be seen near fishing ports such as Pwllheli and Nefyn, near the slate quarries and the mines of Parys Mountain, south Merioneth, and other scattered mines. The large landowners played a major rôle in enclosure, not only enlarging their own estates, but in a number of cases draining formerly useless marshes. As early as the 16th century the Bulkeleys and the Meyricks tried draining and enclosing portions of the Malltraeth Marsh, but the first Enclosure Acts under which 3,000 acres were reclaimed was in 1754–5, a second following in 1788 (the only two 18th-century Acts for Gwynedd). The grand total area enclosed under 19th-century Acts exceeded 7,000 acres in Anglesey, 18,500 in Caernarvonshire, and 4,000 in Merioneth.

More impressive and of continuing value are the reclamations of sea and marsh in the former Glaslyn estuary and the Malltraeth depression. The draining of the latter, though carried out piecemeal over a long period, was only completed in 1811 when the massive dam was built across the mouth of the river Cefni near Bodorgan. Rope and rush mat industries there were based on the local sea grasses, supplied to shipbuilders and later to the railways. Acres of sea marsh were reclaimed. At Pwllheli reclamation made possible the enlargement of its harbour, and in Merioneth Edward Corbet of Ynysmaengwyn, an estate owner with progressive ideas and real concern about the food supply, especially in a period like the Napoleonic Wars, reclaimed over 250 acres of former mossland near the mouth of the Dysynni by drainage and embankment early in the 19th century, and its output was trebled.

A 200-year-old horse plough

94

But the most ambitious scheme of all was the conversion of the Glaslyn estuary to farmland. It had slowly been silting up from the 16th century, yet not one of the early drainage schemes had been carried out. This magnificent inlet penetrated deep into the land, flanked by sheer cliffs on its right bank, and on the other side rising less steeply to the sharp pyramid of Cnicht and the high shoulders of the Moelwyns. Eventually it was William Alexander Madocks, son of a landowner in the Vale of Clwyd and himself an eminent barrister, who was responsible for the planning and execution of this extensive work, and undoubtedly the matter of food supply was in his mind also. Described by Elisabeth Beazley as a practical realist and romantic idealist, he was a man endowed with tremendous mental, nervous, and physical energy, fascinated with architecture and planning and imbued with a deep love of the Welsh countryside. He purchased land in Penmorfa in 1798, drained the area immediately adjoining it the following year, and in 1800, employing 200 workmen, built his first embankment to enclose a stretch of sea sand. In 1801, oats were sown on 1,082 acres of this reclaimed land, followed next year by wheat and rape, and in 1803 by barley and grass. It was then ready to serve as permanent pasture for small Welsh Black cattle such as still graze in this gentle Vale.

Reversible Victorian horse plough

The work continued behind other embankments, drainage being followed by warping and conditioning through a series of croppings. It became possible to provide firm foundations for the little town of Tremadoc, designed by Madocks, and the first planned town in Gwynedd since the days of Edward II. It is still acclaimed by modern planners. It was to have everything! Nestling under the shadow of the old sea cliffs, this charming small place is little more than a village in size. Its market square is at a T-junction with the road along the Vale, part of the Old Caernarvonshire Turnpike. Well-designed shops and houses surround the square, and facing into it on the valley road is a hostelry (now a hotel) and, further on, his town hall with its pillared front. Beyond that again he built a 'manufactory'—a woollen mill powered by water descending steeply from the hills above its source in Llyn Cwm Bach. In addition to the woollen industry and shops, Madocks also provided a fulling mill and a corn mill to give local employment (a school was already nearby for the children), a tavern for the workpeople, and a theatre and racecourse (the latter at Penmorfa) to attract visitors. On the road south from the square he built an Anglican church in the traditional style, and Peniel chapel with a classical frontage. The founding of this Calvinistic place of worship may well have been linked with Madocks' friendship with Howel Harris, the well-known Welsh revivalist preacher. Originally Tremadoc was envisaged as a port, but the harbour and canal failed to materialise, and for some time ships continued to tie up at Ynys Cyngar and unload there. There are many interesting associations with Tremadoc. It was for some time the home of T. E. Lawrence, and among W. A. Madocks' friends were the poet Percy Bysshe Shelley and the evangelist Howel Harris. The granddaughter of Harris's brother Joseph married Madocks as her second husband. Their daughter Eliza Ann Ermine married John Burke Roche who in 1856 became the first Baron Fermoy. Through her mother, who was the Hon. Frances Ruth Burke Roche, H.R.H. Princess Diana is descended from the Madocks and Harris families, and both the Prince and Princess of Wales trace their ancestry from the Royal Line of Gwynedd *via* the Tudor monarch Henry VII.

The first 30 years of the century were to prove critical in many fields. The Napoleonic Wars brought economic turmoil to the countries involved with France, not least to agriculture and trade. Expansion and new inventions were changing the face of industry in Britain, Gwynedd was infected by speculative enterprises in mining, and her quarries humming with activity as the requirement for building materials for new and growing towns in England and South Wales made increasing demands on her resources in granite, limestone, and slate. Turnpiked roads were being built to carry expanding traffic, and the Union of Ireland with Great Britain intensified trade with Dublin, and not least it rendered the Irish mail of vital importance. The ports, large and small, were everywhere developing their facilities and accommodation, especially those facing the Atlantic and Ireland. Men were thinking nationwide and visualising a broad network of roads to serve both internal trade and the ports. In 1806, Madocks was elected Member of Parliament for Boston, and his finger was on the national pulse. The reclamation of the Traeth Mawr was no longer a local project. Competition for the Irish trade brought into renewed prominence the old rivalry for the Irish Mail and on the final choice of a port many schemes for roads across Wales depended. The Post Road to Holyhead still led through Chester and by ferry across to Anglesey. Would Llandudno Bay be a better site for a port to handle it? Others supported the idea of developing Porthdinllaen, a harbour near to Nefyn, to be served by roads crossing Wales, and in 1803 the Portin-llaen Turnpike Trust Act was passed. Three years later the Porthdinllaen Harbour Company was formed. Madocks envisaged not only the construction of a dam across the mouth of the Glaslyn which would make possible a complete coast road around the entire stretch of Cardigan Bay, but saw Tremadoc as a major coaching stop en route to Ireland. At the same time Ynys Cyngar was to be developed as a harbour, and with a new town alongside. He chose an Anglesey man, John Williams, as his estate agent, and although Williams was then only 22, he proved extremely able.

Water mill

96

42. Richard Pennant, Lord Penrhyn (the Thompson portrait). The Ogwen valley in the background.

43. Barmouth and the Mawddach estuary from a print of 1850.

44. Dinorwic quarry, Llanberis. Workshops and Llyn Padern below the now deserted slate galleries.

45. Dinorwic quarry, Llanberis. The sled slope was used to bring down slate from the galleries. Velocipedes below on the railway along the valley.

46. Porthmadog harbour.

47. The Snowdon Mountain Railway near the summit. (*Reproduced by kind permission of Bamforth & Co. Ltd.*)

48. The Festiniog Railway: train passing Llyn Mair. (*Reproduced by kind permission of Bamforth & Co. Ltd.*)

Meanwhile, Madocks petitioned parliament for permission to enclose Traeth Mawr by a great embankment. It would be the first step in the reclamation of over 3,000 acres of estuarine marsh and sand. It was twice rejected, but the Bill was enacted at the third attempt in 1807. This large dam, known locally as the Cob, was designed to link the Merioneth and Caernarvonshire shores between Boston Lodge and Ynys Tywyn. The Ynys Cyngar plan was abandoned in favour of a second new town and harbour, Porthmadog. Some 1,600 yards long and 21 feet high, the Cob would also carry that vital coast road from South Wales and avoid the necessity for a long and unsatisfactory diversion by Aberglaslyn. Between 1803 and 1809 the turnpiked roads to Pwllheli and Porthdinllaen were completed in high hopes which were never to be realised. What had not been foreseen by Madocks was the significance of experiments taking place in steam locomotion, and although the Porthdinllaen scheme lingered on through much of the 1830s, the project was never to come into being. Already, Holyhead harbour works were being extended, and Telford's major North Coast road was completed before Madocks' death. However, the huge task of enclosing the estuary was well advanced by the summer of 1808, with a work force of 200–300 men. Problems were endless, it seemed. The foundations had to be stabilised by under-laying the stonework with rush mats, and the river was diverted to a new course. But at last, in 1811, the gap between the two ends of the dam was closed, only to be damaged by exceptionally high spring tides the following year. It was finally made safe in 1813.

Stanley Mill, Holyhead

The new town of Porthmadog was built at its western end; its harbour diverted the rapidly increasing slate trade of the Ffestiniog quarries from the riverside quays of the Dysynni. Shipbuilding also began, and in 1845, 23,000 tons of slate was exported and 29,000 tons of shipping cleared the port. But Madocks died in 1828, never seeing the fulfilment of his schemes, and it was John Williams who bore all the burden of the later years. The Cob was to carry not only a major link in the West Wales coast road, but many years later, the Cambrian Coast railway. The Festiniog Railway has its old works (Boston Lodge) at the eastern end, and many hundreds of tourists and rail enthusiasts begin or end their journey within sight of it. The Cob is crossed by road each summer by thousands of motorists, all of whom must contribute to its upkeep by payment of a toll. The only exceptions are written into the original contract: any Methodist minister or lay preacher who has to cross (in any vehicle liable to toll) to conduct a service in a church on the other side. History is indeed written into this district and still vividly linked with the present day. The vision and ability of two remarkable men made all this possible, achieving the virtual recreation of this corner of Gwynedd.

XV Slate and the Narrow Gauge Railways

Two great bands of slate cross the mountains of Gwynedd, running from south-west to north-east with the grain of the huge syncline (or downfold) of Snowdon and the ranges to the south. In the northern portion they extend between Nantlle and Bethesda, and in the south from Blaenau Ffestiniog to Penmachno, and still further south they recur through the Corris district. For untold centuries they mattered little except to handfuls of local people who cut the slate to build their cottages and farmhouses. Thomas Pennant travelling through this countryside in the 1780s barely mentioned slate. Yet in 1901, slate accounted for most of over 12,000 men employed in mines and quarries in Caernarvonshire, where it was then the largest occupation group in the county. In Merioneth it was second in importance to agriculture with five short of 4,500 employed, and in the three counties taken together it ranked second to agriculture.

The vast hollow rock basin of the Penrhyn quarries in the Ogwen valley and the colossal slate galleries which terrace the hillsides above Llyn Padarn claim to be the largest quarries in the world, and with them must be classed the long underground mining passages by which slate has long been mined at Blaenau Ffestiniog and many other smaller centres. The processes involved in extracting, cutting, and shaping the slates were the basis of the most important single industry that North-West Wales has known prior to tourism. They now operate, if at all, on a minute scale compared with their former extent, and many are closed. But to gain some idea of the 19th-century industry at its height one should visit the superbly organised North Wales Quarrying Museum at Llanberis where all is now strangely silent, view the carved hillsides there, and make another excursion to the huge hollow of the Penrhyn quarry at Bethesda.

'Cegin' on the Penrhyn Quarry Railway

Developments on a commercial scale began in the latter half of the 18th century—a century which had earlier suffered considerable agricultural depression. In the later decades the interior of Gwynedd had begun to be opened up, and by 1800 there was an incomplete, but nevertheless important, network of turnpike roads. Slate production was still largely in the hands of individual workers who supplemented the meagre income from their limited holdings by small-scale quarrying. Despite this, Ffestiniog increased the output of four quarries from 9,334 tons in 1825 to over 12,000 tons six years later, initiating a

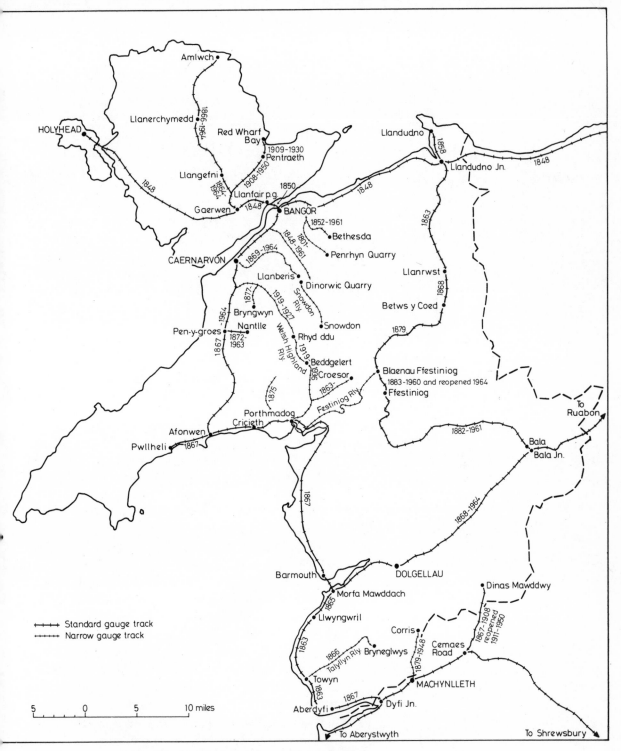

Map 13. Standard and Narrow Gauge Railways.

99

'Chaloner' at the Penyrorbedd Slate Quarry, Nantlle

growing export which started at the little riverside quays, still traceable along the banks of the river Dwyryd, on their journeys to the west coast ports of Glasgow, Liverpool, Runcorn, and Cardiff, and to London and Southampton in the south of England. At the same time, small, scattered quarries in Caernarvonshire were dispatching a mounting tonnage of slate to Caernarvon where, for many decades to come, the busy slate boats were to bring that port to its peak development. Slate was exported as early as 1721 to Dunkirk and Rotterdam, and the clamour for roofing slates later grew in Britain as the building boom rose with the population growth in English, Scottish, and South Wales towns, and especially in the industrialised coalfields. The northern quarries had expanded early, their output exceeding 2,000,000 slates in the 1730s, and double that number, according to the Morris Brothers of Anglesey, were shipped from Caernarvon alone in 1748.

Tools were primitive and transport equally primitive. The quarrymen themselves hauled the slate on sledges as far as the road, and there it was loaded on to carts, or, in some valleys, on to river craft. An advance was achieved by the introduction of blasting powder in the mid-18th century, but the real impetus which made expansion possible came about fortuitously as a result of the marriage of the Cheshire heiress of the Warburtons to Richard Pennant, a relative of Thomas Pennant whose *Tours in Wales* was published in 1778. When Richard's father died in 1781, he inherited the Penrhyn estate just outside Bangor. Thanks to this, to his wife's moiety of the Cheshire estate, and his own natural energy, he launched a vast development of the slate beds of the Ogwen valley. He became Lord Penrhyn in 1783, and a year earlier set himself the task of totally reorganizing his entire estate. The income from the Welsh and Cheshire estates, and from his sugar plantations in Jamaica, enabled him to lease more land, including the foreshore at Pen y bryn and there he created the slate port of Port Penrhyn. With the aid of his very able reeve, William Williams of Anglesey, and Benjamin Wyatt, brother of the architect, he carried out other improvements. Better farming was encouraged, tenants' leases revised, and new houses built for them. More roads were cut on the estate. In the quarrying districts he took over the quarrymen's individual leases and built new houses for them, too, both those who worked in the Penrhyn quarries and those further south in Merioneth.

In 1788, Thomas Assheton Smith, one of the Asshetons of Ashley in Cheshire, also decided on the development of his Caernarvonshire estate of Vaynol, and following Lord Penrhyn's example he began to open up the great slate beds of Dinorwig in the Llanberis valley. Recently J. S. Illsley has linked up the accidental discovery of a flat-bottomed boat found deep in the waters of Llyn Padarn with early transport of both copper and slate as well as passengers from its northern end at Penllyn and from above this point at Cwm y glo on the smaller Llyn Bagelyn to Caernarvon. This *bateau*-style boat discovered in 1977, Mr. Illsley concludes to have been used for slate from the 1780s to, at earliest, the 1820s. So rapid was progress that by 1791 half the slate exports of Caernarvon came from Dinorwig, a total of over 2,500,000 tons. Other pioneers opened up quarries on Cefn du in Llanrug and at Cilgwyn above Nantlle, but the Penrhyn and Dinorwig quarries remained paramount, and continued to produce half the total slate output of the whole of North Wales.

The industry combined with other elements in the economy to stimulate plans for better communications. Newly-made and newly-re-surfaced old roads began to take the place of the rough and muddy tracks of earlier times, so inadequate for the then expanding wheeled traffic. They linked up inland districts, in many cases for the first time, with negotiable routes to the ports and the ferry termini. The old ports were in their heyday and the new slate ports were also carrying on a brisk trade. After Porthmadog was built, its port was soon flourishing with flotillas of slate boats, at the same time as Amlwch was expanding with the copper trade of Parys Mountain in northern Anglesey, and lesser ports benefiting from other mineral ventures. The great weight of stone, ores, and slate also stimulated the designing of faster and stronger ships to carry the heavy loads. It was the great age of sailing ships. At the landward end, the sledges and carts of the first venturers were replaced by horse-drawn waggons on wooden rails. This made it possible to transport slate from quarry to port faster and without break of bulk. In turn wooden rails were replaced by iron ones.

After building the new harbour at Port Penrhyn, Lord Penrhyn turned to other matters. A factory was erected near to the harbour in 1798 and the manufacture of writing slates began there then. Within 10 years 130,000 were supplied to schools all over Britain from this factory, and many new jobs created. Every Victorian schoolboy and schoolgirl used them. In 1800 a road was extended through Nant Ffrancon to Capel Curig, but this did not help to solve the problem of getting slate to the port from the vast quarry in the Ogwen valley on the lower slopes of Mynydd Perfedd. These were the lean years of the French wars when a war tax on slate further distressed the industry, just then expanding rapidly in Snowdonia. Nevertheless, Lord Penrhyn continued to think and plan constructively with a view to the return of peace, and in 1801 he built an iron railway to his new port, the slate drawn to it in trucks by horses. This was the first iron railway of any kind to be built in North Wales.

'Blanche' in Penrhyn Quarry

101

Double fairlie 'Earl of Merioneth' on the Festiniog Railway

Meanwhile Assheton Smith was carrying out parallel work in his Vaynol lands, developing the new harbour of Port Dinorwic at Felin Heli, the old landing-place for the Moel y don ferry, and in 1824 he built a tramway to link it to the Dinorwig quarry. The Peace of Amiens was concluded in 1801 and everywhere it heralded the resumption of economic activity, including a speeding-up in the slate industry. The new quarries being opened up in western Snowdonia at Cilgwyn and Cefn du were served from 1828 by a narrow gauge railway which took their slate from Nantlle to Pen y groes and thence north to Caernarvon. Still more quarries were producing slate in other parts of Caernarvonshire, and from the Crafnant area it was being hauled down to Trefriw from where it was shipped on the river to Conway.

In the first 40 years of the 19th century, nowhere in Gwynedd was the population increase more marked than in the newly-arising quarrying villages such as Nantlle, Pen y groes, and Llanberis. In the Ogwen valley Lord Penrhyn planned a model village 'with no corrupting alehouse'. Quarrymen who had been meeting in farmhouses for worship as Independents seized the opportunity of buying land in the valley which the farmers owned, and there built an Independent chapel which they called Bethesda. It was twice rebuilt and enlarged, and other chapels were erected by these vigorous nonconformists, who were now wage-earning quarrymen. Population quadrupled within half a century, and the town of Bethesda, so utterly different from the traditional settlements of Caernarvonshire, came into being. It was to prove a prototype of villages and hamlets in many parts of Gwynedd, distinctive in appearance and social character. From just under 2,000 in 1821, the population rose to over 7,700 in 1871. It was by then a fully-fledged industrial town. Its long High Street had become its business axis, and the original terraces of small terraced houses had been in considerable part replaced by shops, offices, chapels and public houses. The main housing area moved outwards, with quarrymen's cottages ranged up the hillside. Geraint Davies in a study of Bethesda in that period has described it as a place which had reached maturity, with a wide range of shops, tradesmen, and professional and clerical services and their personnel—such services as banks, insurance, education, etc.—and many of them became resident introducing yet another and better type of housing on the fringe.

Further south on the flanks of the Moelwyns and in the shadow of Cader Idris, two other quarrying districts grew up and became associated with the origin of now famous narrow gauge railways. In the Ffestiniog area slate was used originally, as elsewhere in Wales, mainly by folk who wished to build their own houses. By the early 19th century Casson and Co. were exploiting the area commercially

102

and exporting the slate to British and Irish towns. The finest slates there are the fine-grained grey and blue of the Llandeilo beds found, not on the surface slopes, but at depth and therefore won through adits or by mining, as they were also at Corris. A number of English capitalists were active in exploiting the mineral resources of this more southerly part of Merioneth, and some landowners and developers were involved particularly in the Blaenau quarries and mines. The first exports were carried by packhorses down to the river Dwyryd below Maentwrog. Later in being launched commercially than were the Caernarvonshire quarries, progress was hampered in the early stages by a number of difficulties, but the demand for building materials in the rapidly-expanding towns of England and the growing urban communities of South Wales soon spurred exploitation. By 1832, four quarries were exporting 12,211 tons, most of it shipped by coastal vessels on the Traeth to Glasgow, Cardiff, and the larger English towns. During the early years of the 19th century the extending road network eased transport to some extent, prior to the completion of the great embankment, at Porthmadog. Until then the flat-bottomed slate boats had still to tranship their loads to the Ynys Cyngar quays, and only in 1824 were Madocks's plans for Porthmadog harbour proving viable. By Christmas of that year it could accommodate vessels of 40-tons burden.

The slate trade as a whole, however, badly needed faster and more efficient land transport, and this was particularly the case in Blaenau which is situated high up in mountainous country well away from the coast and with difficult gradients. The town itself is built on steep valley sides, and its situation is far less favourable to urban development than that of Bethesda. Yet this did not prevent its becoming the largest town in the whole of Gwynedd in 1901 with a population of 11,345, just outclassing Bangor. In the 1830s the narrow gauge railway had reached a stage of development at which it appeared to provide the answer to Blaenau's heavy freight traffic. After some delays, a tramway was built across the Cob, and the Act empowering the construction of the Festiniog Railway was passed by parliament in 1832. There was a continuous gradient from the mines to the coast except across a shoulder of the Moelwyns. At first, full wagons came down by gravity. Horses travelled in the van and were used to drag the trains over the Moelwyn rise and again to pull them back to the town empty. The Moelwyns were tunnelled in 1844. By 1850, steam locomotives were being built, and the heavier iron rails which these necessitated were laid first on a 1ft. 11½in. gauge, but this was doubled four years after passengers were first carried in 1865. In 1867, it linked up with the Cambrian coast railway at Porthmadog where sidings were constructed to make this interchange possible.

'Snowdonia' on the Snowdon Mountain Railway

103

'Tal y Llyn' on the Talyllyn Railway

In Merioneth, slate transport was associated with the laying of two other early narrow gauge tracks, the Tal y llyn and the Corris railways. The latter was laid through the beautiful, winding Dulas valley to bring slate from Corris and Aberllefenni in 1858 to meet the Cambrian, later the Great Western main line from Shrewsbury, near Machynlleth. It, too, started with horse-drawn trucks, and steam was not introduced until 1879. From 1883, passengers were carried until 1931, but the quarries, though declining in output, continued to use it for their slate until 1948. The line was closed a year later, after parts of the once lovely valley had become swamped with broken slate waste and turned into a virtual desert.

The Tal y llyn railway has had a happier history. It was opened in 1866 and carried slate from Bryn Eglwys a mile south of Abergynolwyn to the coast at Tywyn, where it joined the Cambrian Railway, later the G.W.R. coast line. Both passengers and slate were carried from the beginning. Despite decreasing freight as quarrying declined, and difficulties caused by two World Wars, its traffic not only continued, but has achieved a record long-term unbroken service for any narrow gauge railway. The slate quarries, which were its *raison d'être*, finally closed in 1946, but this 6¾-mile line from Tywyn Wharf to Abergynolwyn, which served six intermediate stations, was given new life with the formation of the Preservation Society which was incorporated and took it over in 1952. This and the Festiniog Railway, both enthusiastically run by volunteers (and in the case of the F.R. virtually rebuilt by them), make a fascinating chapter of railway history and offer a lesson which is by no means being ignored.

Two of the most remarkable of the narrow gauge railways from the engineering point of view were those built on almost impossibly steep gradients. Of these, the first was the one which replaced the sled slope which originally carried slate down the almost vertical galleries or terraces of the Dinorwig quarry flanking Llyn Padarn. It joined the Padarn railway which ran along level ground from the lakeside to Port Dinorwic. These quarries in the glacier-gouged, dramatically beautiful valley lying in the shadow of Snowdon employed 3,000 men at their busiest, but production dwindled and when they were closed in 1961 the men who therefore had to be laid off numbered only three hundred and fifty. At the height of their working life the quarry area was a large complex with a workshop area round a working yard. The buildings ranged round a quadrangle enclosing this yard now house the North Wales Slate Museum, and original equipment of both the quarries and the railway is displayed in the numerous former workshops. From the discarded railway lines a newly-formed railway company in 1971 rescued the best rails and constructed a tourist line along the side of Llyn Padarn, and within a country park. The Llanberis Lake Railway is now one of the most used of these tourist attractions.

The other is the Snowdon Mountain Railway, built purely for tourists on the rack-and-pinion principle similar to that used on Swiss mountain railways. It climbs in just under five miles to a height of over 3,000 feet at five miles an hour with a limited passenger load of 75 to the Summit station. There are one or two other lines which were custom built for the tourist, such as the Fairbourne Railway on the southern shore of the Mawddach estuary, and a number of now discarded tramways in the resorts. Only one more need be mentioned here, and that is the Welsh Highland Railway. It linked up two earlier ones within its long track of over twenty miles between Caernarvon and Porthmadog. Opening only in 1922, it was closed in 1937, and the rails lifted during World War II. Fortunately this route through the Quellyn valley is now being re-made, as were the Festiniog and the Tal y llyn lines, by volunteer labour, and a return journey over the short portion of the line so far rebuilt became available for the 1982 season.

*   *   *   *   *

The narrow gauge railways and tramways built first for quarry service were a direct result of the exploitation of slate in Gwynedd, and their value to the tourist industry is now very considerable. But to leave the subject of slate and its influence at this point as having introduced new settlements and these specialised railways into the scene would be to do a severe injustice to the human side of the picture. Quarrying, especially on the rock face and in the yards, left ample time for conversation and discussion, and discussion ranged far and wide from literature to music, from politics to religion. A sturdy and highly responsible society with an equally high intellectual and moral fibre resulted, and no understanding of the last 200 years of Gwynedd's history could be complete without taking into account the influence of the folk of these communities. Their work was hard, their days long, and their living conditions far from luxurious. Many succumbed to the dreaded and generally fatal pneumoconiosis, and many were injured at work, but their contribution to Welsh life was great. The hospital was a necessary adjunct to the quarry and a reminder now of the price of slate in human terms. The benefits of the slate industry to Wales must never be forgotten.

XVI The Nonconformists

Bishop Morgan's house

The year of 1564 brought the first significant lightening of the religious horizon in Wales when an Act was passed ordering a translation of the Bible into Welsh. The New Testament was published in 1567, but Bishop William Morgan's Welsh Bible did not appear until 1588, and the first cheap edition only in 1630. On the eve of the 19th century Wales was largely a country of poor peasants dominated by the gentry and served by a Church in which post-Marian Protestantism had resulted in all too little reform. This was in not inconsiderable part due to the fact that Archbishop Laud's *Book of Sports* was of greater influence than the inaccessible Scriptures. Too many clergy failed to discourage Sunday revelry and drunkenness, some of them actually landlords of the inns to which most of the congregation resorted after early Mass on Sundays.

The Elizabethan Church had been rich in scholars and patronage, but there were too few preachers and the Church as a whole failed to integrate with the Welsh or to envisage their needs. Yet the first tender shoots of a re-awakening showed up in the Elizabethan era, giving some hope for a uniform Church. The early 'nonconformists' were the clergy, dedicated men who saw the shortcomings, yet could never have foreseen the changes that the next 300 years were to bring. Despite all the early difficulties and setbacks, the quiet trickles became a river, and the river swelled to a tide so great that in the first decade of the 20th century membership of nonconformist churches in Wales totalled 550,280, the number of communicants in the Established Church in Wales only 193,081. The progress of the virtual revolution is divisible into two phases: the 17th century Puritan Movement deeply inter-locked with the traumatic events of the Cromwellian period; and the Methodist Revival of the 18th century which brought the Welsh flocking into the free churches in unprecedented numbers.

The Puritans as the then 'dissenters' or 'nonconformists' have been termed, clergy who first unknowingly launched the great Movement often described as 'inconformists', hoped to reform the Church from within, opposing many Popish practices and beliefs. They included men such as Rees Pritchard, incumbent of Llanymddyfri (Llandovery, Carms.), and probably only one in Gwynedd—John Williams, vicar of Llandwrog who, despite being taunted, gathered an Independent (Congregational) society, and became an itinerant

106

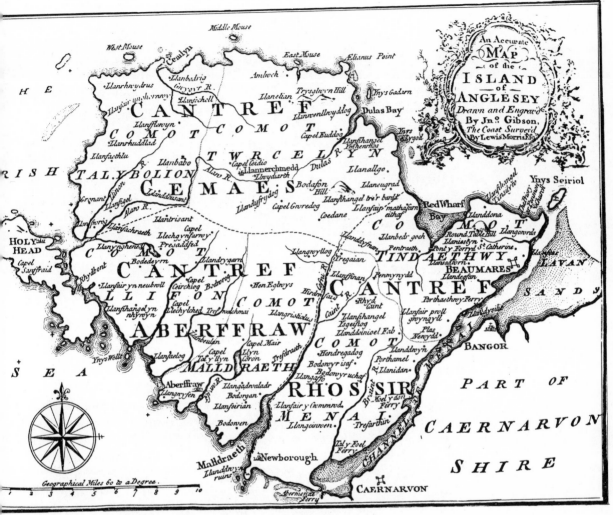

Map 14.—Anglesey, by John Gibson. From Hy. Rowlands, *Mona Antiqua*, 1766 ed.

preacher. Arising in various parts of Wales, the new inconformists were sharply different in their beliefs, some trending one way, some another—Independent, Presbyterian, Baptist, even Unitarian, and yet others still hoping that reform might come within the Established Church. Yet basically all had the common heart and will to bring men and women into a true faith and to holy living. Dissent arose first in the southern Welsh Border counties and South Wales, spread by devoted, fiery itinerant preachers. Their names still ring through Welsh history: men such as William Wroth, the 'apostle of Wales', Walter Cradock, Vavasor Powell, and Morgan Llwyd. Drawing great crowds even in the remoter parts, they were much persecuted, but effected great numbers of conversions during years when, to use Walter Cradock's words, 'the Gospel is run over the mountains as the fire in the thatch'. The Movement extended into mid-Wales and into the north-east, but barely rippled the surface in Anglesey and Caernarvonshire, still remote beyond their massive mountain barrier.

Merioneth alone was deeply affected by the religious influences of the 17th century, and it took the form of strong and expanding Societies of Friends, very different from other nonconformists. It was George Fox, founder of a Quaker group in Yorkshire, who attracted the interest of Morgan Llwyd, a Maentwrog (Mer.) man. At Llwyd's instigation, Fox sent two missioners to Wrexham and Malpas, and in the following year (1654) George Fox preached in Wales, establishing new groups in Denbighshire, Montgomeryshire, and Merioneth. The first adherents are said to have been rough and uncouth, but later ones were typically quiet and upright, deriving their strength as do Quakers everywhere from the Inner Light. Moral standards were high, and family links strong. Yet they were unpopular even with other nonconformists once the first flush of the Puritan Movement faded, refusing to pay church rates or tithes. Persecution was widespread, and to escape it, Quakers emigrated to begin a new life in William Penn's recently-founded settlements in Pennsylvania. By 1700, there were approximately 2,000 people of Welsh Quaker stock in and around Philadelphia, almost half of them Merioneth families. Emigration for religious reasons declined after 1700, but restarted and lasted for 100 years from 1815, many though not all emigrants nonconformists. They contributed considerably to the peopling of Rhode Island, New York state, Philadelphia, as well as to Patagonia and other distant areas. In Wales as in England, a lull in religious fervour occurred during the post-Cromwellian period, but heightened awareness of religious and educational values left a desire for more schools. People were more anxious, and many then more able, to read the Bible in Welsh. The old grammar schools were allowed to function within certain limitations, and in Gwynedd six Propagation Schools were opened.

It remained for the 18th century to initiate a renewal of religious fervour, and it came in full and overflowing measure. Although it was to be known as the Methodist Revival, renewed zeal in reforming the Anglican Church must be taken into account. A confusion of beliefs and practices provided the strange basis from which four major dissenting sects emerged. Yet throughout that emergence there was loyal adherence to the ideals of the early Puritans—the right to differences in belief, freedom of conscience, and strict morality. The way reopened after the 'Glorious Revolution' of 1688 with the accession of the Dutch

Protestants, William and Mary, in 1689. The Toleration Act, passed in the same year, admitted freedom of worship, but permitted the building of Dissenting chapels only with certain conditions. Nevertheless a gate had opened to the way ahead. Until then the different sects had barely begun to take shape: Independents (later to be known as Congregationalists), one of the older Dissents, had survived in small nuclei. In the 18th century the Methodists were added, later divided into two sects—Calvinistic and Wesleyan—the two principal ones in Wales. Progress followed a typical pattern: leadership, the formation of 'societies' accepting a code of beliefs and practice, meetings in cottages and farmhouses, then the building of chapels. From the first, education was an important corollary of the movement, but it was the famous Carmarthenshire clergyman, Griffith Jones, who in 1736 launched the Circulating Schools in Gwynedd, Caernarvonshire heading every other Welsh county with eighty-five. Again itinerant preachers were the early spearhead of the movement, and the age produced the men. Early Puritanism had barely touched Caernarvonshire or Anglesey. Remote from South Wales and the southern Borderland and almost entirely Royalist in sympathy during the Civil Wars, they were the last Welsh bastion to be stormed by nonconformist beliefs. In the 18th century accessibility and means of travel were a major factor in the spread of the new Dissent. The seaways had burgeoned into a resumed prosperity during which West Wales had become dotted with small ports from which sailed ships laden with stone and slate, ores, timber and woollens, returning from ports across the world with fertilisers and general merchandise. Shipbuilding became a major industry in the ports, and in many a small cove along sea and estuarine coasts. Amlwch, Dulas Bay, Redwharf Bay, Beaumaris, and Aberffraw in Anglesey, Conway, Caernarvon, Nefyn, Pwllheli, Porthmadog, Aberdyfi, and Barmouth enjoyed a heyday in the 18th and 19th centuries. Apart from that which led along the north coast and on to Holyhead, the roads of Gwynedd were nearly all rough tracks until the Turnpike Acts for the area were passed after 1800. The establishment and progress of nonconformity were in no small part related to these means of access.

Early Puritan roots were comparatively strong only in Merioneth where Independent groups lingered. Fresh life was given to them when Lewis Rees formed a young society at Llanuwchllyn near the southern end of Lake Bala on the old route across Wales by the Dee valley to the Mawddach estuary. Northward lay the growing slate town of Blaenau Ffestiniog where the new industrial population responded with tremendous fervour to the dissenting preachers, as was the case in all slate quarrying communities. Congregationalism and other dissenting sects spread across the county. The Baptists extended their influence mainly along the coastal belt north of the Mawddach. The Special Baptists and the Scottish, joined before the end of the century to become the Baptists. John Wesley's journeys embraced all three counties on his way to Holyhead and Ireland between 1747 and 1757, but his inability to speak Welsh and the necessity for an interpreter lessened the effectiveness of his words. Although the foundations of Methodism were laid at that time, the building of Wesleyan Methodist chapels in Merioneth began only in the first decade of the following century, most of them in the coastal belt, and four in the north-east, repeating the earlier pattern.

The fourth body of dissenters made the greatest impact in this county and won most adherents. The beginnings of the Calvinists' history here date from the visits of Howel Harris, that great preacher working to win souls at the same time as John Wesley. He started the fire of enthusiasm which, by a fortuitous coincidence, was to make Bala a Mecca of Welsh Methodists. In 1783, Thomas Charles, an ordained priest, came to minister in Bala, met and married a Bala lady, and decided to settle there. Charles was a man of many parts, a powerful preacher, an excellent organiser, and a dedicated educationalist. He veered increasingly towards nonconformity and in 1784 encouraged his Anglican congregation in Bala to link up with the Methodists. He was to become one of the chief founders of the Calvinistic Methodist Church, and in education he promoted Circulating and Sunday Schools. He founded an academy in Bala itself which was the forerunner of the theological College at which hundreds of Calvinist ministers and preachers have been trained. By 1900 there were some 100 churches of this persuasion in Merioneth, well above the number built by any of the three other main nonconformist groups. Daniel Rowland, a leader with Howel Harris of the Methodist Revival in Wales, described Charles as the man who 'gave God to Gwynedd'.

It has long been recognised that from early times Llŷn was more closely in touch with Merioneth than with either Arfon or Arllechwedd. The links were certainly strong in the 18th and 19th centuries in the days of the sailing ships, for apart from the Caernarvon–Pwllheli road, no Turnpike Act provided for better roads in Llŷn prior to 1803. But the distribution of nonconformist churches in the Peninsula up to 1800 outnumbered those in the remainder of Caernarvonshire by three to one because thousands had travelled by sea to Daniel Rowlands' monthly communion meetings in Merioneth, and these people formed the nuclei of early Methodist groups in Llŷn. Only later when better roads became available did nonconformity spread across the rest of the county. A few small Congregationalist groups survived in Caernarvon and Llŷn from the 17th century, meeting in private houses. There were still five such when Howel Harris and Westley visited the district, and again it was Harris's oratory—'thunder was his dwelling place'—which was the most effective, because he preached directly to the people in Welsh. By 1744 he had established new groups in Llŷn and a few in Arfon. Methodism exercised a deep and lasting influence on the quarrymen who flocked to the vast outdoor meetings in the slate and stone quarrying villages such as Llanllyfni and Llanberis, and in the Ogwen valley, as well as many lesser industrial villages in and around the Snowdon Massif. Religious fervour became as infectious in the industrial districts of 18th- and 19th-century Caernarvonshire as it was in the Welsh coalfields. The workmen in the slate quarries took their lunch in rough slate shelters, and the *caban* became the central point for endless discussions on religion, philosophy, education, and politics. Nonconformist chapels, Methodist, Congregationalist, and Baptist, were built with money given by the workpeople, becoming a major element outstanding in the rather drab terraces of cottages and shops. From such towns and villages have come ministers and lay preachers, singers, poets, and politicians. Before the turn of the century there were chapels at Clynnog and Bryncroes, together with a 1799 foundation at Caernarvon. After that, enthusiasm spread rapidly across the entire county, following the turnpiked roads, but chapels were often built just off the road because of danger from vandals.

Anglesey also experienced a momentous revival from 1740, but the first seeds were sown by two laymen before that. William Pritchard, a Llŷn preacher turned out of his farm, was offered one on the Bulkeley estate in Anglesey; and two other local families, the Prichards of Penmynydd, and the Owens of Llanddyfnan, made converts in their own districts. The first nonconformist chapel on the island was built at Mona in 1744, a second at Rhosmeirch in 1748-9, and revivals spread the movement so rapidly that by 1820 the entire island was dotted remarkably evenly with nonconformist chapels. Here, too, Harris and Wesley had visited in the 1740s; so, too, had William Williams of Pantycelyn, no great orator, but the most gifted of Welsh hymn writers and religious poets. His hymns are in every Welsh hymn book, and there can be few English ones which do not include 'Guide me, O Thou great Jehovah'. Williams of Pantycelyn was to Wales what Charles Wesley and Whitefield together were to early English nonconformity.

By 1900 many nonconformist sects were strongly established in Wales, differing in the relative numbers of their churches from one district to another, but from 1800 onwards constituting a joint body of enormous influence. Wesleyan Methodism came more slowly, but it, too, was strengthened in the resorts especially, by large numbers of English-speaking residents who built English Wesleyan churches. Now one of the most characteristic elements in the Welsh settlement scene, the early chapels were large, plain buildings as plainly furbished within, with the pulpit always the central feature symbolising the prime importance of the spoken word. Choirs and hymn singing, and a general lack of ritual characterised the services. The poet-preacher and the scholar-preacher became characteristic, ordained or lay, and there grew up a large body of lay preachers. Nor was their contribution to Welsh life limited to the Church. The democratic government, which is a feature of the dissenting sects, gave experience in organisation and public speaking, and the encouragement of independent thought led to notable movements in the political field, especially in Welsh Radicalism and Liberalism. Gwynedd in particular remembers with pride what David Lloyd George did as prime minister during World War I, and especially for launching social benefits for the retired. A Welsh Baptist, his boyhood was spent in Llanystumdwy and his adult homes were in Cricieth. It was, in fact, nonconformists who were largely responsible for getting through parliament the Act for disestablishment of the 'Church of Wales' as it became from 1920, and without doubt the Church itself had benefited from the reforming lessons of the Dissenters. Education was an active field of nonconformist vigour and its members were prime movers in the founding both of non-denominational teacher training colleges and the first Colleges of the University of Wales, those at Aberystwyth and Bangor.

Peniel chapel, Tremadoc

All over Wales, the chapel-manse-Sunday School complex is an intimate part of both the landscape and social life. Many of the older chapels bear scriptural names such as Salem, Carmel, Hebron, Bethesda, and Nasareth. Industrial hamlets of the chapel-building period in many cases took their names from them. These names are broadcast now over the map of Gwynedd and, together with *Capel,* mingle with the *Llan* and *Betws* names of an earlier religious vintage. By 1882 there were some 700 chapels in Gwynedd alone, exercising a fundamental influence on public morals and ways of life. True, by 1914, the fervour had reached a height never since attained, and membership and church attendance alike have dwindled severely. Many chapels have even become redundant. But no-one can hope to understand Gwynedd or any other part of Wales who fails to appreciate the contribution that nonconformity made in 200 years to the whole character of Wales, its language, and its people. Equally important was its influence on the moral, educational, and political fronts.

9. Howel Harris.

50. The Reverend Thomas Charles of Bala.

51. Garreg Congregational chapel and manse, Merioneth. A characteristic rural Nonconformist 'complex'.

52. South Stack lighthouse.

53. Holyhead Harbour from the *Station Hotel*, September 1905. SS. *Anglia* and SS. *Galtee Moor* berthed.

Porth Dafarch, Holy Island.

55. Holyhead: the parish church of St Cybi. This fine medieval church lies within the walls of the Roman fort.

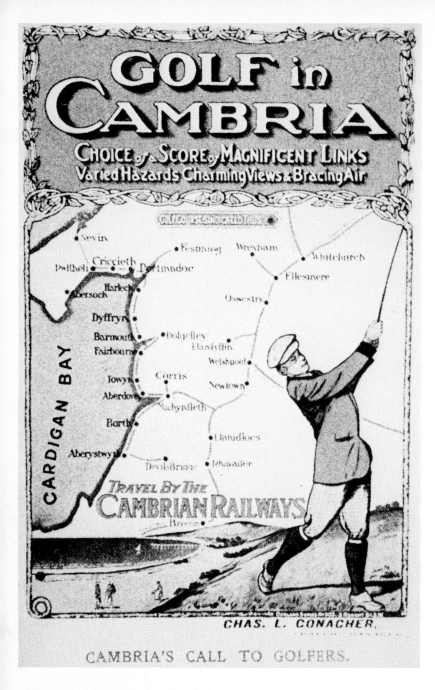

CAMBRIA'S CALL TO GOLFERS.

56. (*left*) A Cambrian Railway poster of 1910 advertising the delights of the north Cardigan Bay coast to golfers.

57. (*below left*) Llandudno: part of the splendid sea front with the Great Orme as background.

58. (*below*) Dolgellau, Eldon Square. Dolgellau was the county town of Merioneth prior to 1974.

XVII Holyhead and the North Coast Railway

'Here is a small market kept on Saturday, for the convenience of the town, and passengers that travel this way to and from Ireland.

'The number of houses or families, town included, is 240, and the number of souls about 1400.'

Cambrian Register, 1818

The sea links between Dublin and North Wales became commercially as well as politically more important after the Union of Great Britain and Ireland in 1800. Trade was also mounting and the competition for the Irish mail continued, with Holyhead, Porthdinllaen, Liverpool, and St George's Harbour (in Llandudno Bay) as the contenders. Speed was essential for the mail; so were good port facilities. The road from London to Liverpool was shorter, but the sea voyage, which was the slow part of the total journey, was roughly double that from Holyhead which is only some 70 miles from Howth where Rennie's harbour works were then in course of construction to serve Dublin. There was also brisk sea trade between Liverpool and North-West Wales during these years when the slate output was mounting, and granite, limestone, and ores were exported from Gwynedd's ports as well as wool and dairy produce. The small ports were involved from the 18th century, and as the sea lanes became more crowded, Trinity House became increasingly concerned for the safety of vessels in a storm. Lighthouses were a matter of urgency. The rocky islets of the Skerries had been equipped with a light as early as the reign of Queen Anne, the only one prior to the building of the Point Lynas light in 1781. Holyhead harbour's followed in 1808, and the South Stack lighthouse was erected at a point under the shadow of Holyhead Mountain, most difficult of access for its builders, during the following year. It not only served to warn shipping of the dangers of the jagged cliffs and headlands of the Holy Island coast, but acted as guide for the mail boats which for some four years made for Porth Dafarch when they could not safely enter Holyhead.

The new Steam Packet Co. operated seven packet boats from Holyhead in 1819, replaced by Post Office paddle steamers during 1820. Improvements to the harbour were urgent, for Lewis Morris's charts show the Holyhead coastline as still entirely natural in the mid-18th century, and it was little different in 1802 except for the

'Scotia' at Holyhead, 1905

113

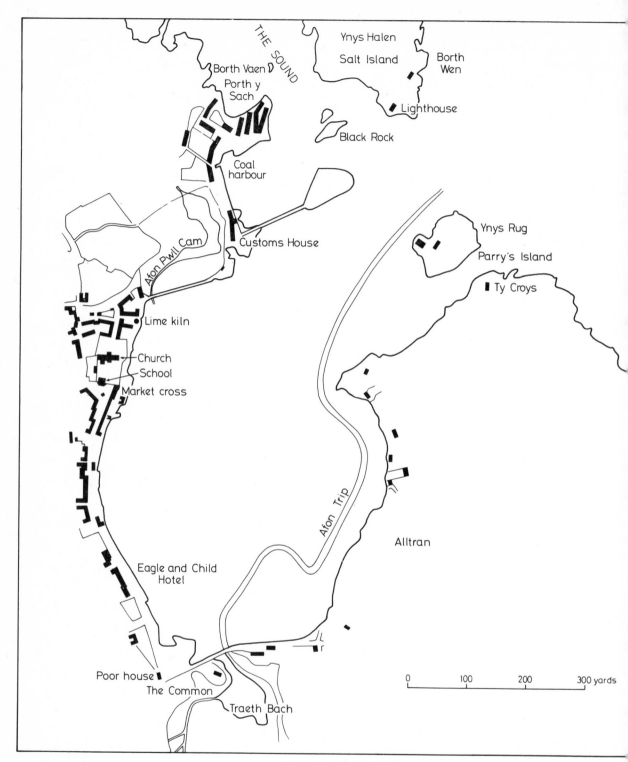

THE SOUND

Ynys Halen
Salt Island

Borth Wen

Borth Vaen
Porth y
Sach

Lighthouse

Black Rock

Coal
harbour

Afon Pwll Cam

Customs House

Ynys Rug
Parry's Island

Ty Croys

Lime kiln

Church
School
Market cross

Afon Trip

Alltran

Eagle and Child
Hotel

Poor house
The Common

Traeth Bach

0   100   200   300 yards

Map 15. Plan of Holyhead, 1802.

114

light on Salt Island. Yet Holyhead has the great advantage of deeper water than any other roadstead between the Clyde and Milford Haven. In 1838, the rail link between London and Liverpool was completed, and to Holyhead's chagrin, the mail was transferred to Liverpool in that year. It was the sharpest reminder that the improvement of her port facilities was a matter of urgency, and secondly and even more essential, she must ensure that this new and revolutionary type of rail transport be swiftly planned and built to connect her with the capital. By 1838 the marriage of the new broad gauge permanent way with fast and powerful locomotive haulage had already been amply proved to be practical, efficient, and potentially profitable. Holyhead got to work at last, and with the Crewe–Chester rail link already under way, several schemes were put forward for its extension across North Wales.

Robert Stephenson

The Crewe–Chester line was opened in 1840, and in 1842 Robert Stephenson's plans for a Chester–Holyhead railway were approved. Railway mania was at its height, when the permitting Act for the Chester Holyhead Railway was passed in 1844, and Robert Stephenson was appointed engineer. Some of the problems of construction along this coast had become familiar in relation to road building, but railway levels demanded even more complex planning. The line was constructed simultaneously in different sections. Three long bridges had to be built—over the Dee, the Conwy, and the Menai Straits; the headlands at Llanddulas and Penmaenbach tunnelled, but the task of tunnelling Penmaenmawr was too great and instead, the permanent way was built out from below the near-vertical seaward edge of the mountain on a stilt-like series of supports. To compensate both the initial cost and that of constant surveying and maintenance, journeys including these and other difficult sections of the line are specially costed. Over 12,000 men were employed at a time during much of the building programme as well as hundreds of horses and their drivers to deliver materials and to cart away spoil as the line was cut.

The first train passed over the Conwy bridge in April 1848 and in that year Holyhead regained the mail traffic. The Anglesey section of the route was completed at the same time, but only one tube of the Britannia tubular bridge was then finished. Horses hauled waggons over the Menai bridge to join another locomotive on the far side and passengers crossed by road until both were ready. The first through London to Holyhead train made the journey in this way on 31 July 1850, leaving Euston at 8.45 p.m. and arriving at Holyhead's wooden station platform at 6.45 next morning. The time taken for the journey was dramatically reduced from the 48 hours taken by the mail coach in 1784, and was soon to be even shorter. Track laying across the island presented relatively little difficulty; only one tunnel had to be cut (near Bodorgan), and the crossing of Beddmanarch Bay was simplified by the existence of the Stanley Embankment. The line entered Holyhead alongside Telford's road. With Britannia bridge completed, rigid timing was enforced because of the Royal Mail, by then restored to Holyhead, and a fine imposed for every minute the train ran late. The night Irish Mail left Euston at 5.00 p.m. in 1850 arriving in Holyhead at 1.05 a.m., 8 hours 5 minutes later; a boat express leaving Euston at 9.00 a.m. arrived at 5.15 p.m., that is in 8 hours 15 minutes, calling at some intermediate stations, the timing reduced by about an hour once the bridge was in use. The number of passengers increased from 189,000 in 1848 (May to December inclusive), to a peak of 767,000 in 1855. Ten trains did the journey each way daily between London and Holyhead from 1855–1860, and letters posted in either London or Dublin in the morning were delivered in the other capital that evening. A Post Office van sorted mail on the train, and letters were picked up at scheduled intermediate points direct into the van as the train continued non-stop.

The *Cambrian Register* figure for Holyhead's population in 1818 was an underestimate, for the 1801 Census recorded just over 2,000. Nevertheless, the description of a small market town coincides with the character of this minor port and fishing centre as it was in the early years of the 19th century. The 1802 Plan depicts a straggle of cottages around the tiny market place adjoining St Cybi's parish church, running down the slope of Market Street, and a few fishermen's and seamen's dwellings clustered on the small headland opposite Salt Island. The best known building other than the church was the *Eagle and Child* (later the *Royal* hotel), long a resting-place for road travellers waiting to sail to Ireland including Jonathan Swift and John Wesley. The successful fight to retain the mail traffic initiated swift and unprecedented growth, and by 1901 its population had risen to over 10,000, a figure which has remained fairly steady ever since.

Holyhead owes its rise to its position geographically so advantaged for the Irish crossing to Dublin, and the railway which serve its 19th century port. It became a principal transit point between Britain and Ireland, and development of its harbour facilities followed, but the construction of the Chester and Holyhead Railway, later absorbed into the L.N.W.R., alone made possible the Holyhead of today. Freight traffic, though considerable, failed to stimulate any significant industrial development, apart from ship repairing. It remained to a marked degree a packet port, and as such a transit point, with consumer industries of a minor character except for the provisioning of boats sailing from its port and express trains carrying long-distance passengers to and from the capital. The construction of the railway was accomplished within five years, except for the completion of the Britannia tubular bridge. Port developments spanned nearly seventy years. During that period, labourers and engineers, architects and builders swarmed into the town. The mid-century Irish famines provided a ready supply of labourers and the early basis of the considerable element of Irish in the town. An Act of 1810 permitted improvements in parts of both Holyhead and Howth harbours, though later Kingstown replaced Howth as the port of Dublin. The Admiralty Pier, built between 1810 and 1824, linked the north-west corner of the deep inlet with Salt Island, measuring 1,150 feet by 50 feet. A second pier and a graving dock were also built, and the wide cleft in the coastline which was the estuary of the little Afon Trip was deepened. This wide inlet, which could shrink to nothing more than a mud flat at low neaps, was to become the new inner harbour and give superior shelter to shipping during gales. No longer would it be necessary for vessels to run to Porth Dafarch in such weather. Additionally, it would match up with the accommodation in the new harbour at Kingstown which in 1834 took over from Howth, and provide safe harbourage for the new fleet of Post Office paddle steamers.

The 1850 Britannia Tubular Bridge

By 1837, Holyhead was able to begin ship repairing, its main industry until 1971. However, despite the new Admiralty pier which Rennie built, the draught alongside was still insufficient for large vessels to tie up there at low tide when it could fall to 10 feet. Another problem was the desirability for passengers between train and boat to find both alongside, and led to the further deepening of the Inner Harbour. An Act of 1847 provided for the extension and improvement of the harbour, and in 1851 the second station was built. By this time, steamboats had reduced the crossing time, the number of passengers had increased, and more overnight accommodation was needed. In 1859, the L.N.W.R. was in control of both railway and shipping and much of the construction work. The large *Station* hotel was erected in 1880 at the entrance to the station and landing stage, and in 1873 they had recognised the need to extend the docking and wharfage facilities on the Turkey Shore where ship repairing was carried on. This was in large part resultant on the final major project—the creation of the Outer Harbour as a Harbour of Refuge. This enormous undertaking was achieved by the building of a giant breakwater 7,860 feet long. Begun in 1848, it took 25 years to complete using stone from Holyhead Mountain and from Penmon, and employing 400 workmen. The result was the superb deep water Harbour of Refuge which can shelter a large number of ships of any size and draught. Sadly, the station has now been reduced in effect to two platforms without the usual

117

*Irish Mail nearing
Conway Tubular
Bridge*

appurtenances, and the impressive *Station* hotel was demolished in 1979. However, a new station precinct is planned.

The recreation of this superb shoreline into a modern port, together with many other adjuncts proper to it and a broad sea front promenade, have made a magnificent sea frontage. The town behind it has remained undistinguished, and since 1900 has failed to expand, keeping within the 10–11,000 bracket. The lairages are empty, and the cattle trade is reduced to transit only since the introduction of containerisation in the 1970s. The town has lost by this latter innovation, and the A5 is overburdened. But the apparent failure of Holyhead to achieve continuous growth needs a second look. It will then be seen that although rocks are everywhere near the surface, except in local hollows, they are carved up into Holy Island's beautiful north-west coastal headlands and coves, and inland give rise to elevated sites which afford wide views of sea and shore. These features have attracted new settlement outside the old town, and Trearddur Bay in Holyhead Rural C.P. now houses a considerable suburban population and provides hotel and other accommodation for large numbers of summer visitors. In 1891, Holyhead Rural recorded a population of eight hundred and sixty-five. For 1981 the preliminary figure is 3,573, and Holyhead Urban remains little changed at 10,427. The rise in Anglesey's population which has taken place steadily throughout the present century is in no small part due to this type of growth in many parts of the island, yet the Census figures still fail to reflect this additional tourist residence during the summer months.

XVIII   The Towns of Gwynedd

It was 1189 when Giraldus Cambrensis visited Gwynedd, and his dictum that 'The Welsh . . . have neither towns, villages, or castles', so true for Gwynedd, was to remain so for almost another 100 years. It was the last Welsh stronghold that the English kings had failed to conquer. During the 13th century, although Gwynedd's rulers were copying the feudal pattern in some ways, and had built more effective castles, none was associated with appreciable concentrations of population. But there are indications that village nuclei were developing at a few places, for example at Llanfaes, Nefyn, and Pwllheli. Strictly speaking, a town was synonymous with a borough, and a borough only created by charter. Among its usual provisions were the privileges of self-administration and the holding of markets, and this was the case in the castellated boroughs, those intrusive urban communities discussed with others in Chapters Nine to Eleven. Yet Gwynedd still only opened slowly to external influences. By the late 13th century, England had widely distributed country markets, most of them the core of country towns, and in 1310, Edward II decreed that only in its six castle towns (including Bere), could markets be held in Gwynedd, *except* that goods might be sold locally at places so distant from these towns as to be unable to take advantage of their markets. Anglesey certainly seized on this opportunity, and from 1346 markets or fairs were being held at Aberffraw and Llanerchymedd. But progress was slow, and although the accession of the Tudors helped to open Welsh eyes to wider possibilities, real commercial progress was halting and limited. The drovers extended trade contacts especially during the two following centuries, but the rise of local market centres and the development of the small ports took place on an appreciable scale only in the 18th century.

A major urban revolution in Gwynedd was a feature of the 19th century, a complex of cause and effect already illustrated in the case of the slate towns and Holyhead (Chapters Fifteen and Seventeen). There were many others, and they transformed, even though on a comparatively modest scale, the urban map of this reluctant region. Growth was uneven, typified in some by unevenness, even by decline, or by sharp spurts of growth or re-growth. They were not only varied in their economic basis and physical aspect, but there was an incredible leap-frogging as first one and then another town claimed first place.

Cambrian Railway Orion bus, Pwllheli to Nefyn, 1906

119

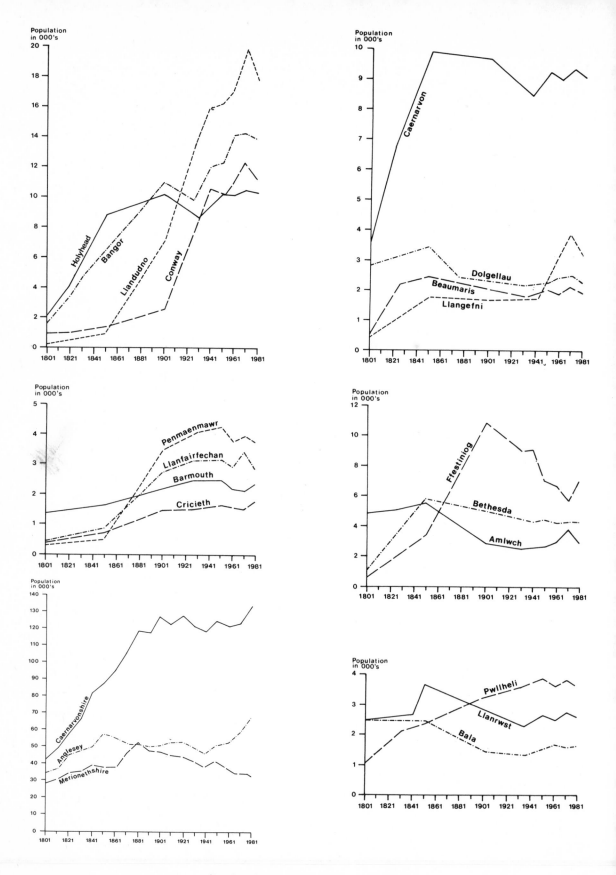

Graphs of Urban Population in Gwynedd.

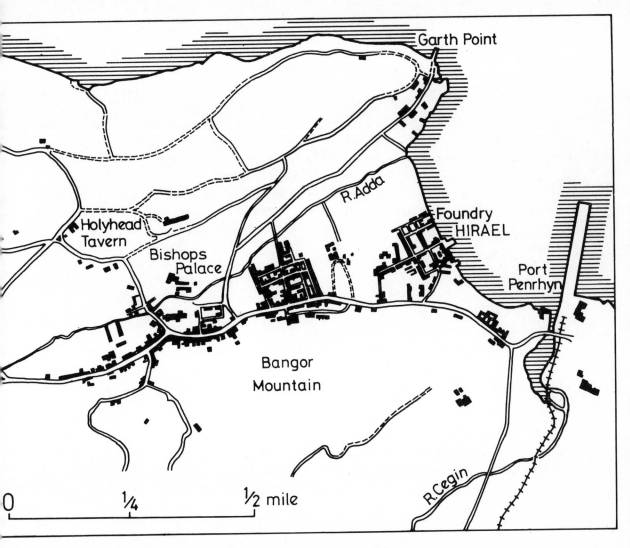

Map 16. Plan of Bangor, from the Tithe Map, 1840.

For the most part they were associated with rising prosperity and population, but in administrative terms it was in transition, and order only emerged with the passing of the Local Government Act of 1894 which bestowed the status of municipal borough on five of Gwynedd's towns, and that of urban district on another group of lesser centres. The 1972 Local Government Act unfortunately ended this tidy urban structure, but the designation of these 22 as towns (less Corwen, but with the addition of Llanrwst as county boundaries were altered) has been retained in the 1981 Preliminary Census Returns. Hence it is possible to construct graphs of population for every town either from 1801 or from the date when it became recognizable as an entity

121

T.S.M.V. St Sillio, *1935,*
at Llandudno

in the Census Returns, until 1981. No attempt is here made to follow a strict classification, but grouping and divergences, and their general character as urban centres are central to the descriptions which follow. And again there emerges the age-long importance of sea communications and coastal location.

There is a possibility that one day archaeologists may find, say, near *Segontium,* another *Maridunum,* but that eventuality apart, **Bangor** has prime claim to be Gwynedd's oldest urban foundation. Much remains to be learnt about this cathedral city and its diocese, but it is assumed that it was founded by St Deiniol in the 6th century. Coming to this place from Bangor is y coed, he found it to be near the sea, but sheltered against sea rovers' raiding by the ridge on which are now built Upper Bangor and the University College of North Wales. It is a site typical of those chosen for Celtic religious houses. Always looked upon as their particular cure, the diocese is significantly co-extensive with the Gwynedd of the princes. There are no known remains of monastic buildings, and the cathedral, built on the same site, has more than once suffered burning and wilful destruction, notably by Owain Glyn Dŵr. Rebuilt once again by Bishop Deane in 1496, much of that building was carefully restored and retained in the reconstruction by Gilbert Scott in 1866 and by Caroe a century later, both preserving the tombs of Owain Gwynedd, of one of the Tudor family, and a memorial to the Welsh poet, Goronwy Owen. In 1801, Bangor was a city of only 1,770 souls. Today it is North Wales' most important educational and scientific centre, with U.C.N.W., three Colleges of Education, and the ancient foundation of Friars' School. The economic upturn in the Ogwen Valley stimulated its growth in the early 19th century, to be further advanced by Telford's road and the Chester-Holyhead Railway and their vital bridges across the Conwy and the Straits. Long a place of transit for Holyhead and the Irish crossing, its inns multiplied. It caught the first flush of the summer visitor tradition, and built more hotels. Now the cathedral stands at the heart of a busy commercial area, near to the fine modern buildings of U.C.N.W., and in term time Bangor numbers within its boundaries a population which may substantially exceed the Census figures, the latest of which (1981) record just short of 14,000. Now Gwynedd's second largest town, it has remained so since the First World War.

Apart from Bangor, the Edwardian castle towns rank as the most ancient, and of these, only Harlech fails to qualify as urban. Of the remaining four, Caernarvon and Beaumaris were created shire towns. **Caernarvon** was not only the principal one, but remained the largest in Gwynedd during much of its history. Always pre-eminent in administrative status, it is now more so as the 'capital' of the new county of

122

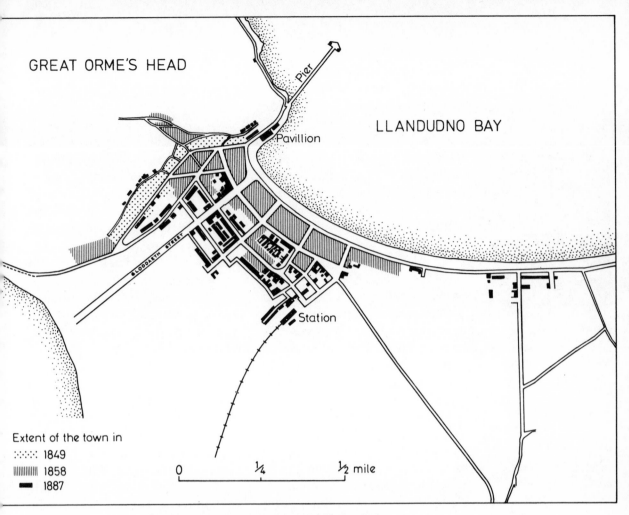

GREAT ORME'S HEAD

LLANDUDNO BAY

Pier

Pavillion

GLODDAETH STREET

Station

Extent of the town in
:::::: 1849
|||||||| 1858
▬ 1887

0 ¼ ½ mile

Map 17. The Early Development of Llandudno.

Gwynedd. Edward selected well for his times, but today, it stands on the extreme western edge of the most developed part of Gwynedd. Communications with the north coast of Llŷn have never been good, and since the Beeching closures, it is disadvantaged by having no rail link—an absurdity for a county town of so large an area. In the early 19th century it was beaten into second place in size by Amlwch, after having long been the largest. Nevertheless, the slate trade of its own hinterland gave shipping on the river Seiont a sharp boost, and, as slate boomed and rail and road transport improved, Caernarvon had regained its lead by 1851, experiencing an almost threefold increase to 9,883 inhabitants. It suffered defeats in the population stakes later, but from 1901 it has remained steadily around 10,000. Administrative centrality, regional market and shopping services, are added to the tourist attractions of the great castle and *Segontium,* both kept in superb condition by the Ministry of Environment. Apart from the

123

castle, the market place, the walls, and the harbour, it is unremarkable as a town, but its outlook across the Strait and its hinterland are both beautiful. Today the Slate Quay is demoted to a car park, and flanks a deserted river once so crowded with shipping.

Conway, by contrast, survived merely as a small port housing only 889 people in 1801, and only 2,504 in 1901, its fisheries and coasting trade alone of any significance despite its road and rail links. From the 1920s it then made an enormous leap ahead, almost quadrupling its population by 1931 to 8,872. Since then it has increased further to 12,206 in 1971, its peak figure. Two causes may be adduced: the growth of Degannwy across the estuary as a residential area, and Conway's own praiseworthy efforts to develop a tourist trade. Although there are no sea-front hotels in the old town, it must be accorded outstanding beauty and great historical attractions. These are now admirably exploited, but its main charm lies in its wide estuary, a perfect setting for the famous bridges leading the eye up to the towering walls of the castle rising high above the quayside, a scene made colourful with fishing smacks and pleasure craft.

Beaumaris, castle town, ferry terminus, and long the county town of Anglesey, was swiftly deprived of its through traffic with the construction of the two bridges across the Straits. From 1826, the North Coast road ran eight miles to the east, leaving Beaumaris at the T-junction of what had become minor routes, its port long since silted up. But it had already a clientèle of 'carriage folk' who came to stay at its elegant hotel on the smooth stretch of the Green. Its now assured quietness brought dividends. With a tally of only 574 inhabitants in 1801, growth unexpectedly followed to nearly 2,500 by mid-century. During the early years of this century it ceased to be a county town, but a pleasing countryside, the perpetually changing panorama of the great heights of Snowdonia across the Straits, and the rare beauty of the moated castle, have continued to keep the little town prosperous ever since. Meanwhile, **Menai Bridge** arose as a bridge-head settlement on the site of an old ferry terminus after 1826 and is now a town of over 2,000.

Llangefni, as a hamlet of a few stone cottages, in 1785, took over the market function of Llanerchymedd 13 miles to the north. It drew some benefit from the small Malltraeth coalfield hamlets nearby for much of the 19th century. In addition it stood on the Post Road, and a branch railway, now closed, except for freight, ran through from Gaerwen to Amlwch. The town once founded spared no pains. It was determined to grow, and with a certain centrality in the Island and a population of 1,700 to 1,800, the County Council meetings were held there from 1899. It later became the county town in place of Beaumaris. Its urban history lies wholly within the last 200 years,

Llandudno and Colwyn Bay Electric Railway Ltd Tramcar

124

and during that time it has vigorously developed its educational facilities and attracted new industries. Reaching a population figure of almost 4,000 in 1971, it has become the efficient administrative centre of what is now the Borough of Ynys Môn or the Isle of Anglesey.

Dolgellau, the third of the former county towns, passed its peak as a woollens centre in the latter half of the 19th century, and now, like Llangefni, administers Merioneth without County status. This little town is a cluster of houses and shops, stone built amid massive mountains. Although not on the main coast route, it is a centre for climbers, nearby Cader Idris their main attraction. Two other former woollen towns, **Bala** and **Llanrwst,** also declined with the loss of the cloth trade to Yorkshire after the mid-19th century. Bala then with a population of two and a half thousand, Llanrwst with three and a half thousand, both losing about one thousand inhabitants, and then altering little until recently. True country regional centres with market functions, with road and rail and a rich valley, each providing shoppers with facilities in pleasant mature settings, each full of history. Bala within the last few years has developed its High Street, and has attractive hotels, restaurants, and many shops, and Llanrwst, around its market square, has all the fascination of a mountain and forest background.

The three towns which are dependent on extractive industries have had mixed fortunes. Only Bethesda and Blaenau Ffestiniog among the slate-quarrying centres reached urban status, for, of its large workforce, many commuted from nearby towns and villages. In 1851, Bethesda ranked fourth in Gwynedd with a population of almost 6,000, ahead of Amlwch, the copper export port, which by then was in fifth place. Bethesda reached its peak in 1871 with 7,739 inhabitants, and after that, as slate output fell, slid gently down to the 4,000 range, where it has remained, a now mature and stable community since World War Two. But **Blaenau Ffestiniog** peaked in 1901 at 11,435, almost 50 per cent. over Bethesda's maximum population. Just ahead of Bangor, it was for a time the largest town in Gwynedd, but it, too, declined sharply when its slate industry collapsed, dropping to 5,751 in 1971. From being a successful industrial centre, the inland terminus of the Festiniog Railway linked at Llandudno Junction to the main North Coast line, it suffered depopulation and severe unemployment, remote and grim amid its great mountains, its very atmosphere spelling desolation and despair. But within the last decade it has shown its mettle, refurbishing the valley by shifting huge quantities of disfiguring slate waste, re-soiling and replanting it, and developing the Llechwedd Caves as a tourist enterprise. It has built new houses and gained 1,000 residents. The future still bears a question mark, but the major pumped

Cambrian Coast line at Harlech

125

Ty Crwn, Barmouth,
a 19th-century gaol

storage scheme at its door attracts 40,000 tourists a year, and the Festiniog Railway brings thousands more. It is a town that dare not lose hope.

Amlwch, the third of the towns which rose—and fell—on the basis of mineral extraction, is now experiencing a second rise. As the outlet for Parys Mountain's copper ores from the later part of the 18th century, in 1801 its inhabitants numbered 4,977—1,350 more than the next largest town, Caernarvon. By 1851 it achieved 5,813, and then its copper workings ceased for all practical purposes. It fell rapidly to under three thousand by 1901. Its second chance was aided by tourism and an attractive setting in north Anglesey (population 3,682 in 1971). Now, as the Anglesey Marine Terminal for Shell U.K., it has a further prospect of development. With an offshore draught of 120 feet, and the most modern mooring buoy in its bay, it is suitable for 70,000 dwt. tankers to moor and discharge their crude at all times. The old rock-walled harbour is not affected, and a shore station at Amlwch pumps the oil to a tank farm at Rhosgoch, three miles away. There are residents now in new buildings, the harbourmaster, H.M. Customs, and the Pilotage Authority and marine support groups. A committee controls the port and includes a majority of representatives nominated by the Anglesey Borough Council and the Amlwch Community Council, as well as those appointed by Shell U.K. and Liverpool Pilotage Authority, all of whom are deeply interested and active in its planning and development. The residential and tourist elements contribute to its re-growth.

Finally, the railway facilities which did so much for the development of Holyhead, gave rise to numerous seaside resorts and recreated old ports in that rôle. Along the north coast where open coasts, sandy beaches, invigorating air, and natural beauty of coast and hinterland offer so much to holiday-makers, have risen **Penmaenmawr** from a minor hamlet in Dwygfylchi parish, and its neighbour **Llanfairfechan.** Both were concerned previously only with exporting the granite of Penmaenmawr Mountain prior to the building of the railway. Now they have grown into small attractive towns of over 3,000; and in the case of Penmaenmawr, topping 4,000 in 1951. Along the coast of Cardigan Bay, the Cambrian Coast line together with the Great Western Railway, connected this part of West Wales to the West Midlands, between 1863 and 1867, and had similar effects. It not only assisted the growth of Porthmadog as port and shopping centre, but virtually recreated the small ports of **Aberdyfi, Barmouth, Tywyn,** and **Pwllheli,** and the old castle town of **Cricieth,** re-casting them in a new rôle, and their size ranging from 1,500 to 4,000 at the present day.

But the star example is **Llandudno,** for half a century the largest

126

town in the three counties, 19,077 its peak population in 1971. It does not compare with the large English resorts in size, but that it does so in high-class hotel accommodation is evident from its selection as their meeting place by so many large national conferences. Gogarth on its west shore was given by Edward I for a bishop's palace. The only settlements for centuries afterwards were miners', seamen's and quarrymen's cottages on the Great Orme. Much of the site of today's town was sea and salt marsh, part common grazing, wide, windswept, and desolate, until it was reclaimed by the Mostyns of Gloddaeth. Swift development began with the plans of Edward Mostyn, M.P., and Owain Williams, an Anglesey architect, in 1847. The 1848 Enclosure Act created 955 allotments, an area of 822 acres earmarked for the Mostyns, and this was the land on which the town was built very swiftly from that date. The population rose from only 318 in 1801 to 1,131 in 1851. The main thoroughfare, Mostyn Street, and the first town hall were ready before 1854, quickly followed by the sea front hotels. The present pier succeeded earlier ones in 1876, and Marine Drive around the white cliffs of the Great Orme was completed in 1878. Streets, houses, and hotels alike were well planned, and by the 1870s extension began in Craig y don near the Little Orme, and the West Shore developed mainly in the 20th century. The railway line from Llandudno Junction reached the town in 1858, and rapidly increasing numbers of family visitors and many distinguished holiday-makers flooded in. By the 1920s it had overtaken every other town in Gwynedd, 'carriage folk' and middle-class railway travellers alike swarming into luxuriously equipped and serviced hotels or into boarding houses and apartments. With a population of 19,177 in 1971 it is 4,500 ahead of its nearest rival, Bangor. The age of the car serves it equally well, as does the fame of its shops, for Mostyn Street has emporia of more London firms than any other street outside the capital. Only by climbing to St Tudno's little church high up on the Great Orme can one be at the ancient site of the earliest Llandudno, see the superb expanse of Llandudno Bay, and the now spreading town built on once empty marshland.

St Tudno's church, Llandudno

XIX The Twentieth Century

THE LEAN YEARS

Power line, Nant Gwynant

The pendulum of Time swings for all countries and peoples, for all regions and many industries. On account of large areas of infertility and limited raw materials, combined with distance from markets, Gwynedd has been particularly liable to suffer in times of depression. In the past, only minerals and sheep have offered a living in many parts of Snowdonia, and by the 20th century, gold, copper, silver, and lead ores were either worked out or uneconomic to mine in most of Merioneth and Caernarvonshire. Hence the large-scale development of the slate industry from the late 18th century proved an economic saviour. But during the 1890s boom and slump alternated and labour troubles sparked off serious strikes. The worst occurred in the Penrhyn quarries early in the 20th century, lasting three years and bringing terrible hardship to Bethesda. The consequent shortages of slate on the market brought in French imports of up to 40,000 tons annually for a period of over five years. Men were being dismissed from the quarries before 1914, and at the onset of war many joined the armed forces. Few wished to earn a living in the quarries when they returned. Edward Pennant had succeeded to the Penrhyn estate, and after 1911 he built new sawing and dressing sheds and introduced electrification at Penrhyn quarry, but despite a brief boom in the '20s, the industry was in recession again during the depression of the '30s. The building boom of the '40s after World War Two saw a flood of cheap ceramic tiles produced, and slate for roofing went out of fashion. Prices fell, and more men were laid off. Between 1898 and 1918, the U.K.'s slate output fell from 668,589 to 110,000 tons; its best subsequent figure was 221,000 tons in 1922. Some quarries were sold, for example, the Oakley, and the Llechwedd in Ffestiniog was closed. Eventually the Dinorwic quarries finished all production, and 2,000 men were dismissed. In 1901, the total employed in all Gwynedd's mines and quarries was 20,000. It is now some three thousand.

So important was this group in Caernarvonshire in 1901 that it exceeded those in agriculture by 50 per cent.; the number in agriculture almost doubled those in transport, and these were easily the three largest groups. In Merioneth the agriculture and the mining and quarrying group were approximately equal. In Anglesey, however, although it is only about half the size of Caernarvonshire, there were

128

59. Llandudno: a Bedford photograph of *c.*1900, when development was beginning in Craig y don.

60. The Happy Valley, Llandudno, *c.*1900.

61. Gwydyr Forest: 'sympathetic planting' in the rugged terrain round Llyn Crafnant.

62. Anglesey Aluminium Metal Company's Works in their setting near Holyhead town.

63. Ffestiniog pumped storage station. The oblique aerial photograph shows Llyn Stwlan in its glacial *cirque* or *cwm* and the pipe line linking it and the Tan y Grisiau reservoir which feeds it from below.

64. Maentwrog hydro-electric station in the Vale of Ffestiniog.

65. Trawsfynydd atomic power station and the artificially created lake, the waters of which are used for cooling.

only 1,000 fewer in agriculture; its second largest group in communications and transport, mainly railwaymen, and dock workers and seamen. Looking at the three Gwynedd counties as a whole, one searched in vain for figures of any significance through which cash income might come from outside the region, apart from ores and slate, and the meat, wool, and hides from animal feeding. Such manufacturing groups as are recorded were almost all supplying goods related to agricultural or quarried products or, in modest numbers, to the building and construction trades and consumers' normal requirements.

When other output flagged and failed, agriculture maintained its basic importance, Anglesey the most productive of the three counties, yet hardly any of its land ranks as grades one and two. Thin soil cover and ill-drained hollows are numerous; nevertheless, there alone do arable land and permanent grass constitute the bulk of the farmed land. On the mainland both types are largely confined to the better coastal and valley lowlands. Cereals are now rarely sown in Merioneth, but both northern counties harvest barley and oats from better drained soil areas, barley mainly now for animal feed, oats of diminishing importance. Stock farming is dominant everywhere, and although the drovers have long been but a memory, beef cattle, usually Hereford crosses, provide most farmers' money income except in the true hill farms. Dairying is only of significance in the richer land, that is, principally in Llŷn and Anglesey. Friesians are favoured in northern and western districts, and considerable amounts of surplus milk are sent to North-East Wales and England, quantities over and above that requirement made into cheese and butter at local factories as at Llangefni and Chwilog.

LAND USE 1971

Acres

	Anglesey	%	Caerns.	%	Merioneth	%	Gwynedd	%
Arable	30,728 ⎫		32,199 ⎫		18,381 ⎫		81,308 ⎫	
Permanent grass	96,065 ⎬ 80.8		87,019 ⎬ 55.65		76,746 ⎬ 27.03		259,830 ⎬ 47.7	
Rough grazing	15,991 ⎭		83,569 ⎭		19,069 ⎭		118,629 ⎭	
*Total farmland	142,784		202,787		114,196		963,174	
†Forests *circa*	3,800	2.1	122,970	6.35	25,350	6.0	52,120	5.4
All other land	30,110	17.1	138,351	38.0	282,826	66.97	451,287	46.9
Total area..	176,694	100.0	364,108	100.0	422,372	100.0	963,174	100.0

*Ministry of Agriculture Annual Returns.   †Estimate based on Forestry Commission figures.

129

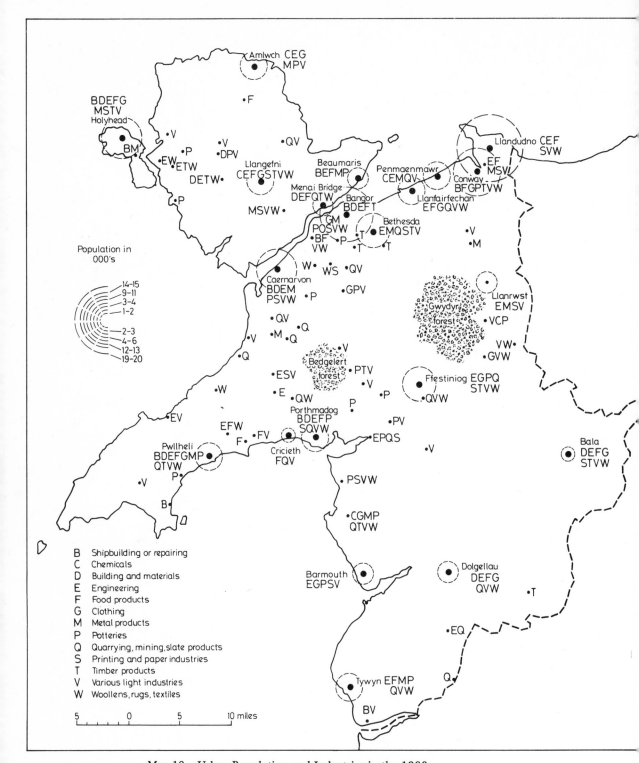

Map 18. Urban Population and Industries in the 1980s.

Sheep are the life blood of the upland farms, less so of the mixed farms, and in Anglesey they are widely grazed on the well drained, drier pastures. The Welsh Mountain breed predominates on the mainland, though in Llŷn large grass sheep are preferred. The age-old custom of wintering mountain sheep in the lowlands, often at some distance away, is now confined to one-year-old lambs. Were the mixed farms to raise more rape and turnips, wintering might be dispensed with altogether. In Gwynedd, meat and wool are both money crops, and crossing with Down breeds is not uncommon. Welsh wool has a low shrinkage rate and is in demand by knitters and weavers, and traditional patterned Welsh coatings and tweeds now have a wide sale. Throughout the upland farms, the shepherds' life is also traditional—fairs, markets, sheep courts, competitions, and the shearing at which neighbours' help is mutually given, break the otherwise lonely routine of the upland shepherds. It is they who have to face the searing winds, the mists, and the bitter cold, and when snow lies white for weeks on the high peaks, and sheep are lost, life is hard indeed.

Pine marten

Gavelkind, by which the old law gave shares of property to all heirs, has long since passed, but in practice many smallholdings survived long afterwards, until at last they failed to support their owners. Most have been absorbed into larger farms, but ruined cottages and broken stone walls still bear witness to times when dire poverty led to emigration or to seeking work in the towns. The smaller number of holdings in part explains the decrease in the numbers engaged in agriculture, now down from first place in numbers employed; there were 20,500 in 1901, 2,700 in 1978. But the change is too drastic to be explained by that alone and two other developments are also responsible. The first is mechanisation; the second follows from that, for the farm labourers are largely dispensed with, and the family alone runs many farms. The financial benefits are clear; buildings, house, furnishings and decoration, and the standards of dress and way of life are noticeably superior to those of a few decades ago.

The weakness in Gwynedd's economy, however, became increasingly evident. Once slate had gone into serious decline, manufacturing industries became almost wholly limited to the needs of the local society: consumer goods, building and construction, and supplies for these and for such transport as passed through the area. The tourists were still largely in the coastal resorts, and as more travelled by car, the railways' income was reduced and railmen were employed in smaller numbers. At the same time, professional, commercial, banking, and defence elements in the population were increasing as the producers of goods declined. The '60s brought the Beeching cuts. A number of lines were axed, and on main lines the number of stations reduced together with the frequency of services; which was cause and which result a matter of dispute. The rural areas were most affected once again, the position of the urban communities one of growth. In 1901, the employment groups comprising professionals, banking, scientific, and those in administration and defence was 7,586. By 1978, they totalled over 20,000. In addition, appreciable numbers of retired folk were becoming residents, most of them from England. The standard of living was rising throughout the country, and very necessary public supplies of water, gas, and electricity were in demand in the extending suburban fringes of the old towns. The numbers employed in these services rose from 140 in 1901 to 2,680 in 1978. There were bonuses, but in this too lay nothing which could be sold outside the region. For too many years Gwynedd's economy had been limited to one of maintenance.

THE WAY AHEAD

Day to day and year by year, this largely non-progressive economy had gone on through wars and depressions. Miracles were desperately needed to stimulate the flagging structure, and there seemed no hope of these. Yet they were already stealing across the horizon unrecognized, and the first came in the very guise of defeat. Britain's timber reserves were the lowest in Europe, and the onset of war in 1914 found her desperate for supplies which shipping, facing an enemy blockade and most needed for food, was ill equipped to carry from overseas. Fully alert at last to the serious extent of deforestation, discussions and conferences led to the *Forestry Act* of 1919 as a result of which the Forestry Commission was born. The State at that time owned only 70,000 acres of Crown woods; the Forestry Corps numbered only 15,000, and 90 per cent. of our timber requirements were being imported annually. By 1942, the number of forestry workers had doubled, and timber from home woods was up by 50 per cent.

The first land was acquired in 1920. Planting was to be confined to terrain which would otherwise be used only as rough grazing, so the suitability of large acreages in Wales, Scotland, and the north of England was obvious. The first land was taken over that year, some of it on the old Gwydyr estate on the eastern slopes of the Snowdon Massif, to the west of the Conwy. The first band of workers recruited were necessarily unskilled in woodmanship, many of them local ex-miners and quarrymen, and training the workforce was the first hurdle. There were many other problems and difficulties. Land had first to be cleared, weeded, and fenced against pests such as mice, voles, rabbits, foxes, and nibbling sheep. Paths and, later, roads had to be made, accommodation provided for staff and woodmen, nurseries set up to raise the first saplings for new plantings, and tests then carried out on soils, and experiments made to find which trees would adapt to different soils, slope, altitude, and aspect. The forester's main fear is fire, and a constant watch must be kept. Many varieties of conifer were tried: Douglas fir, European larch, silver fir, Western hemlock, and in time broad leaf trees were planted as amenity near the forest margins. Profitability only came when trees reached the age for economic felling, but much was felled during the Second World War from sheer necessity. Now there is a rich variety of trees; wild fauna and flora are protected as far as possible, and mechanisation has reduced sheer physical labour. A new social element has been established, many workers living in the wooden bungalows of hamlets built by the Commission. The forests now extend over most of the eastern slopes of Gwynedd's vast mountain core from Gwydyr, Beddgelert, and Lledr forests south to Coed y Brenin. By 1965, 9.75 per cent. of Wales was wooded, and Welsh forests comprised 11 per cent. of the British total. Now slopes which were once bare rock are richly clothed with woodlands which enhance even the beauty of these great mountains, their lake shores and their valleys.

The public's response to this new forest environment was one of unexpected enthusiasm. They walked, they climbed, they picnicked. As a result all Gwydyr was designated a Forest Park in 1937, and the need both to provide for its requirements and guard against possible dangers such as fire risk and damage to young trees and fences was also recognized as essential. Planning and conservation became the operative words, for not only was there great beauty in this park, but within its bounds historic monuments, great houses, rare flora and fauna. As far back as 1895, a property behind Barmouth had been donated to the National Trust, formed in that year, and now the owner of many valuable and historic properties. Slowly the idea of a Forest Park led to thoughts of a National Park, and the National Parks Commission was set up in 1949. There was a convergence of purpose between the three bodies as to the need for conservation. The original Forest Park is now incorporated in the Snowdonia National Park, a vast area extending over Gwynedd's central mountain ranges from Conway south to the Mawddach and the Dyfi, and including in its bounds the great forests, the Forest Park, National Trust properties, many antiquities, quarries and old mine workings, and the industries and settlements of the 25,000 people living there. The National Park Authority designated in 1951 does not own property. Its limited financial resources are devoted to such matters as an information service and consultation with other interested bodies with parallel interests. Its 90 permanent staff and 10 wardens co-operate with the

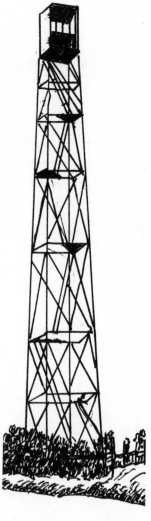

Firetower in the forest

133

A lake fringe in the forest

Forestry Commission, and it is the planning authority for the area within the Park in consultation with Gwynedd County Council. It also works with the National Environment Research Council, the National Conservancy Committee for Wales, the Development Board for Wales, and the National Society for the Protection of Rural Wales, and has responsibility for the Nature Reserves within the Park, and has set up visitors' centres.

Catering for and accommodating the now large numbers of visitors who have discovered the pleasures of the Park, has extended Gwynedd's tourist industry to almost all the mainland area. Climbers, country walkers, those with specialised interests in the environment, educational groups, and many others now visit it in thousands every year. As a result, places such as Beddgelert, and Betws y coed have blossomed into small inland resorts. The Wales Tourist Board has published expert research studies of the economic aspects of this rapidly expanded industry, now a major contributor to Gwynedd's economy. In 1982, it reveals, Gwynedd had 72 per cent. of all Welsh serviced accommodation, 25 per cent. of all farmhouse letting, and a total of 22,000 caravan pitches. In 1971, of all tourist spending in Wales 41 per cent. is credited to North Wales as a whole, which is reported to have 550 hotels and guest houses. The main season lasts a bare four months, but good weather may afford it a modest extension. Because much employment in catering and tourist accommodation is seasonal, it suits many housewives, and 60–75 per cent. of all females employed are accounted for in connection with the tourist industry. The exact numbers employed or the total income derived from tourism, directly and indirectly is impossible to assess. There are day visitors. Food, transport, souvenirs, admission fees, and even more basic needs such as clothing and footwear, household and personal goods are purchased. But the Wales Tourist Board estimates put the number of 1973 visitors to Gwynedd as 2.77 million, and the income so derived as £41 million. The roads are overcrowded as a result. New roads are needed, and an extension of the Express Way (from Chester along the North Coast) beyond the river Conwy is now under discussion. But the narrow gauge railways do a brisk business. They carried 1,252,000 passengers in 1971, and 1,125,000 in 1981, the Festiniog Railway heading the list in both years. The map of industries shows how widely rural workshops and factories are now spread across Gwynedd, especially concerned with the manufacture of woollens, pottery, leather goods, small wooden items from love-spoons to stools, and metal ware from costume jewellery to household gadgets. In this new tourist era, tourism serves Gwynedd's expanding industry, and her industries serve tourism.

There is no longer doubt that Gwynedd has wakened to the necessity of extending her manufacturing industries. In Anglesey, Llangefni has been vigorous in such promotions, and Menai Bridge deserves mention also. Caernarvonshire leads in this respect with numerous concerns in Pwllheli, Porthmadog, Caernarvon, Bethesda, and Conway, in addition to a wide scatter in lesser towns and villages. But Merioneth is still lagging behind, though Blaenau Ffestiniog is a notable exception, like Bethesda a slate town fighting to maintain and renew itself. The message has reached Bala, Dolgellau, and Tywyn which are entering the small industries scene, but particular mention may be made of Llanbedr, a village which has achieved notable advances in establishing small industries. Power has always been lacking in Gwynedd, water and sheer human manipulation apart. Its insignificant coal resources, now neglected, did little for Anglesey's economy and that only briefly. Now with the age of electrical power advancing into nuclear and hydro-electric stations, generation in Gwynedd is on a scale which offers hitherto undreamed-of possibilities. Early town electricity stations burnt coal to produce power: Llandudno from 1895; Bangor, 1897; and Caernarvon, 1902. Hydro-electric production began after the formation of the North Wales Power Company in 1904. The first station was built at Cwm Dyli in 1906, followed by Dolgarrog a year later, and Maentwrog in 1925. It was still impossible to supply remote rural areas with public supplies of water, gas, and electricity in the '40s and '50s. Hydro-electricity could be produced nowhere more effectively than in Gwynedd's high mountain core with its ample rainfall; and streams and lakes are full all the year round. Altitude and heavy precipitation became transformed into the potential miracle the region needed. A nuclear power station was built at Trawsfynydd and completed in 1965 with a man-made lake for cooling. It is the last Magnox-type nuclear-powered station to be built in Britain. A more advanced principle, that of pumped storage was introduced with the building of the Ffestiniog station at Tan y grisiau, near to Blaenau in 1961–3. Such generation depends on there being two lakes or reservoirs, one at a level high above the lower one. Water is pumped from the lower to the upper and released when it is required to turn the turbines which operate the generators. Glaciated mountains with a high rainfall and suitable lakes or hollows are ideal. At Ffestiniog, a small lake, Llyn Stwlan, in a glacier-scooped *cwm* was deepened, enlarged, and contained by a controlling dam, and an artificial lake made far below near-vertical heights. Power is fed daily into the national grid. Begun in 1974, the largest pumped storage station in Europe is nearing completion at Dinorwic, near the now deserted slate galleries of Llanberis. This massive and ambitious scheme also

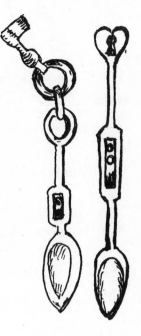

Traditional North Welsh love spoon

135

uses a deepened *cwm* lake, Llyn Marchlyn, and the natural glacial valley lake, Llyn Peris, 1,640 feet below. Unlike Ffestiniog where the fall from the upper lake is a surface fall, at Dinorwic the released water will descend through a vertical shaft 1,450 feet deep to turbines linked by hydraulic tunnel to Llyn Peris. The gouging out of these massive underground tunnels has meant the removal of some three million tons of solid slate. The scale of civil engineering work involved is colossal, including also the building of high level approach roads to Llyn Marchlyn, laying pipe lines, and the subsequent landscaping of the site. It requires a very large labour force and, at the request of Gwynedd County Council, 90 per cent. are locally recruited. Once completed, its function will be primarily that of a booster station able to supply extra power to the grid at a moment's notice in emergencies or peak periods. All such stations dependent on water power have the great advantage of being cheap to operate. In addition to work opportunities during construction, numerous components are being made locally, and there will be permanent long-term jobs on completion. This incredible achievement and Gwynedd's other power stations are a miracle of environmental adaptation and usage, making available power for future possibilities as yet not even envisaged.

A happy example of industrial renewal has been made successful by Penrhyn Quarries, Ltd., a member of the Marchwiel Minerals Group. A controlling interest was obtained in 1964 from the Penrhyn Estate after 200 years of ownership by the Penrhyn family. Now the quarries are wholly owned by the company which is known as Penrhyn Quarries, Ltd. After mechanisation and modernisation, quarry production has risen again, totalling 345,000 tonnes a year. The slate may be processed in one of four ways. Roofing slates are cut mechanically into any number of sizes according to customer requirements, instead of the traditional countesses, duchesses, ladies, and doubles. Secondly, an architectural department offers advanced designs in slate of many colours and shades for large and small building projects—wall facings, wall blocks, flooring, paving, and other uses. Both are supplying a widening market, including West European countries and the United States. Thirdly, pulverised slate, so graded as to provide any required degree of fineness, commands the second biggest market for Penrhyn's products. It is used in a wide variety of medical and cosmetic preparations. In addition this fullersite dust can form a constituent part of bitumen products, plastics, resins, and finishes for roofing felts. In coal-tar enamel it prevents rust when painted on undersea piping. Lastly, the six square miles covered by slate waste serve as a quarry for slate crushed to form the basis of roads. The entire road can be constructed with it except for the surface finish. When the road deck was built above the railway of the rebuilt Britannia bridge following the disastrous fire of 1979, Penrhyn slate was used in this way. This product absorbs 300,000 tons of slate waste a year. All machinery at Penrhyn is operated by electricity instead of water power, greatly reducing manual labour.

The Anglesey Aluminium Metal plant at Holyhead was opened in 1971, and is the most important industrial concern on the island. Attracted by Holyhead as a deep water port, the power resources of Wylfa, and fast rail and road travel, its very modern works are at Penrhos, where it has rail links, and a tunnel from its own jetty is used to transport the white alumina powder from port to plant. Linked with two international companies, Kaiser of the U.S.A. and Rio Tinto Zinc, it has a maximum capacity of 112,000 tonnes per annun, and, at this maximum production, can employ 1,360 people. The versatile, non-magnetic metal demands production involving electrolysis, some processing requiring a continuous 24-hour shift system. Once the alumina is reduced, the molten aluminium is cast. Because of its light weight, it is widely used in the manufacture of cars, ships, and aeroplanes, in the electrical industry, for foil and cooking equipment, and window and door frames. In addition to the works site, the company owns an adjacent farm with a herd of Canadian Holsteins and a large flock of sheep, and a wild life nature reserve on Holy Island. It is not only Anglesey's largest employer, its significance lies in the use it makes of Holyhead's port and of Wylfa's power.

It is appropriate now that the story of Amlwch's oil terminal should be put in its wider setting, that of its link with Shell U.K.'s refinery at Stanlow. This, too, is a farsighted project. This, too, demonstrates Gwynedd's extending links with the rest of Britain and highlights her widening space relations. Both Penrhos and the oil terminal have seized on the deep water facilities off Anglesey's northern ports, her electric power resources, and good long-distance communications, envisaging as did the C.E.G.B. the potentialities of the region. The pipe-line is 75 miles long, and crosses the Straits and three large river valleys. All these projects are completed by careful attention to the landscape. In them, the pioneering spirit of the 19th-century road and rail builders is seen again. Moreover, the centuries-old shackles of remoteness are diminished and the barrenness of Snowdonia'a high altitude core in economic terms has been broken. The work of the National Park Authority and many other bodies, and the Local Authorities, together have brought tourists flooding in. Now the C.E.G.B.'s pumped storage schemes, and those of industrial groups are showing the way ahead for further ventures, and crowning this success, Gwynedd's economic new dawn is no longer just a dream beyond the horizon.

Rare Snowdon lily

Welsh Glossary

abaty, abbey
aber, mouth or confluence of river
afon, river
ardal, district
bach, nook, end, small
bangor, consecrated land, monastery
bedd, grave
betws, chapel of ease
blaen, blaenau, head, end, upland
bod, abode
bryn, hill
bwlch, pass, gap
bychan, small
caban, cabin, hut
cadair, cader, seat, stronghold
cantref, *cf.* English hundred, district
caer, fort, camp
capel, chapel
castell, castle
cefn, ridge
celli, grove
clas, mother church, collegiate church
coch, red
coed, a wood, trees
craig, crag
crib, summit
croes, cross, cross road
crwth, Welsh violin
cwm, valley, corrie
Cymru, Wales
Cymry, the Welsh
din, hill fort
dinas, hill fort, city
drwg, pass, gap
du, black
dwr, dwfr, water
dyffryn, valley
eglwys, church
esgob, bishop
ffin, boundary
ffordd, road
ffridd, sheep walk, high pasture
ffynnon, spring, well
glan, river bank
glas, green, blue
glyn, glen, valley
gwaun, moor, mountain
gwely, literally, a bed, hence family,
    settlement
gwlad, country
gwyn, white, fair
hafod, summer dwelling
hen, old

hendref, old township, permanent
    winter settlement
heol, hewl, road
is, below as in Is Gwynedd
llan, place, usually church place, hence
    church in place-names
llanerch, glade
llech, stone, rock
llyn, lake
llys, palace, prince's dwelling
maen, stone
maes, plain, open field
mawr, big, great
melin, mill
moel, bare hill
morfa, marsh, seashore
myn, ore, mine
mynachlog, monastery
mynydd, mountain
nant, stream, vale
newydd, new
nos, night
pandy, pl. pandai, fulling mill
pant, hollow, valley
parc, park
pen, head, end
pentref, hamlet, end settlement
perfedd, middle
plas, hall, mansion
plwyf, parish
pont, bridge
porth, port
pwll, pool
pystyll, waterfall
rhaeadr, waterfall
rhaglaw, government officer
rhiw, hill
rhos, moor
rhyd, ford
rhyngyll, beadle
sarn, causeway
sir, shire
tir, land, territory
traeth, strand, shore
traws, cross, district
tref, township, town
ty, pl. tai, house
ty'n llan, vicarage, rectory
uchaf, upper
ynys, island
ysbyty, hospital
ystad, estate

Dynasty Table

DYNASTY OF GWYNEDD

	died		died
Rhodri Mawr	878	Gruffydd ap Cynan . .	.1137
Anarawd	916	Owain Gwynedd . .	.1170
Idwal Foel . . .	942	Llywelyn ap Iorwerth (the Great)	1240
Meurig	986	David	.1246
Idwal	996	Llywelyn ap Gruffydd .	.1282
Iago	1039		

KINGS OF ENGLAND

reign	Anglo-Saxon	reign	Plantagenets
1042–66	Edward the Confessor	1154–89	Henry II
1066	Harold	1189–99	Richard I
		1199–1216	John
	House of Normandy	1216–72	Henry III
1066–87	William I	1272–	Edward I
1087–1100	William II		
1100–35	Henry I		
1135–54	Stephen		

ENGLAND AND WALES

reign		reign	
–1307	Edward I	1399–1461	House of Lancaster
1307–27	Edward II	1461–1485	House of York
1327–77	Edward III	1485–1603	House of Tudor
1377–99	Richard II	1485–1509	Henry VII
		1509–47	Henry VIII

N.B. The above rulers are selected to relate to the text.

Bibliography

Only published volumes are included in the following list. Many very important studies are to be found in the regular publications by county and national societies, and readers wishing to pursue any subject further are advised to consult their *Transactions.*

Alcock, Leslie, *Arthur's Britain,* London, 1971.

Black's *Picturesque Guide to Wales,* Edinburgh, 1856.

Bassett, I. M. and B. L. Davies, *Atlas of Caernarvonshire,* Caernarvon, 1977.

Baughan, Peter, E., *The Chester and Holyhead Railway,* Newton Abbott, 1972.

Beazley, Elisabeth, *Madocks and the Wonder of Wales,* London, 1967.

Beresford, Maurice, *New Towns of the Middle Ages,* Lutterworth, 1967.

Bowen, E. G. (ed.), *Wales,* London, 1957.

Bowen, E. G., *Saints, Seaways, and Settlements,* Cardiff, 1969.

Bowen, E. G. *Britain and the Western Seaways,* London, 1972.

Bowen, E. G., and Colin Gresham, *History of Merioneth,* Vol. I, Dolgellau, 1967.

Bowen, Geraint, *Atlas Meirionydd,* Bala, n.d.

Campbell, Bruce and Richenda Scott, *Snowdonia,* London, 1949.

Carter, Harold, *The Towns of Wales,* Cardiff, 1956.

Christiansen, R., and R. W. Miller, *The Cambrian Railways,* 2 vols., 1969.

Collingwood, R. G., and Ian Richmond, *The Archaeology of Roman Britain,* London, 1969.

Condry, W., *The Snowdonia National Park,* Fontana, 1968.

Davies, Henry Rees, *A Review of the Records of the Conway and Menai Ferries,* Cardiff, 1942.

Davies, Walter, *A General Review of the Agriculture and Domestic Economy of Wales,* Board of Agriculture, 1813.

Defoe, Daniel, *A Tour through the Whole Island of Great Britain, 1724-26,* Everyman, 1962.

Dodd, A. H., *The Industrial Revolution in North Wales,* Cardiff, 1933.

Dodd, A. H., *A History of Caernarvonshire,* Denbigh, 1968.

Dodd, A. H., *Life in Wales,* London, 1972.

Edwards, Sir J. Goronwy, *The Principality of Wales, 1267-1967,* Caernarvon, 1969.

Emery, F. V., *Wales,* World's Landscape Series, London, 1969.

Evans, G. Nesta, *Social Life in Mid-Eighteenth Century Anglesey,* Cardiff, 1951.

Foster, R. Ll., and Glyn Daniel, *Prehistoric and Early Wales,* London, 1965.

Giraldus Cambrensis, *Itinerary through Wales* and *Description of Wales,* Everyman edition, 1908.

Gresham, Colin A., *Eifionydd,* Cardiff, 1973.

Grimes, W. F., *The Prehistory of Wales,* Cardiff, 2nd edn., 1951.

Godwin, Fay, and Shirley Toulson, *The Drovers' Roads of Wales,* London, 1977.

Hall, Edmund Hyde, *A Description of Caernarvonshire, 1809-11,* Caernarvon, 1932.

Houlder, C. H., *Wales: An Archaeological Guide,* London, 1974.

Howell, David W., *Land and People in Nineteenth Century Wales,* London, 1978.

Hughes, D. L., and Dorothy M. Williams, *Holyhead, the Story of a Port,* 1967.

Hughes, Emrys and Aled Eames, *Porthmadog Ships,* Gwynedd Archives Service, 1975.

Jenkins, J. Geraint, *Life and Tradition in Rural Wales*, Cardiff, 1969.

Jones, Francis, *The Princes and Principality of Wales*, Cardiff, 1969.

Jones, Gwyn, and Thomas Jones, *The Mabinogion*, Everyman edition, 1949.

Jones, R. Brinley (ed.), *The Anatomy of Wales*, Peterston-super-Ely, 1972.

Jones, Richard B., *British Narrow Gauge Railways*, Vol. IV, *Welsh Railways*, London. 1958.

Kay, George, *The Agriculture of North Wales*, Edinburgh, 1794.

Lewis, E. A., *The Medieval Boroughs of Snowdonia*, Cardiff, 1912.

Lewis, H. Elvet, *Nonconformity in Wales*, London, 1912.

Lewis, Samuel, *Topographical Dictionary of Wales*, 2 vols., London, 1833.

Lindsay, Jean, *A History of the North Wales Slate Industry*, Newton Abbott, 1974.

Lloyd, J. E., *A History of Wales from the Earliest Times to the Edwardian Conquest*, London, 1911.

Lynch, Frances, *Prehistoric Anglesey*, Llangefni, 1970.

Milward, Roy, and Adrian Robinson, *Landscapes of North Wales*, Newton Abbot, 1978.

Moore, Donald (ed.), *The Irish Sea Province in Archaeology and History*, Cardiff, 1970.

Morgan, D. W., *Brief Glory*, Liverpool, 1948.

Nash-Williams, V. E., *The Early Christian Monuments of Wales*, Cardiff, 1950.

Owen, G. Dyfnallt, *Elizabeth Wales: the Social Scene*, Cardiff, 1962.

Owen, Hugh, *The Life and Works of Lewis Morris*, Anglesey Antiquarian Society and Field Club, 1951.

Pierce, T. Jones (ed. J. Brinley Smith), *Medieval Welsh Society*, Cardiff, 1972.

Pennant, Thomas, *Tours in Wales*, 1773–81 (ed. John Rhys), 3 vols., Caernarvon, 1778 and 1883.

Rees, Thomas, *History of Protestant Nonconformity in Wales*, London, 1861 and 1883.

Rees, William, *An Historical Atlas of Wales*, Cardiff, 1951.

Richards, Melville (ed.), *An Atlas of Anglesey*, Anglesey Community Council, Llangefni, 1972.

Roderick, A. J. (ed.), *Wales through the Ages*, 2 vols., Llandybie, 1959 and 1965.

Ryle, George, *Forest Service*, Newton Abbot, 1969.

Shaw, Donald L., *Gwydyr Forest in Snowdonia: A History*, Forestry Commission, 1971.

Thomas, Brinley, *The Welsh Economy*, Cardiff, 1962.

Thomas, David, *Agriculture in Wales during the Napoleonic Wars*, Cardiff, 1963.

Thomas, David, *Cau'r Tiroedd Comin*, Liverpool, n.d.

Thomas, Hugh, *A History of Wales 1485–1660*, Cardiff, 1962.

Waters, W. H., *The Edwardian Settlement of North Wales in its Administrative and Legal Aspects, 1284–1343*, Cardiff, 1935.

Watson, Katherine, *North Wales*, Regional Archaeology Series, 1965.

Williams, A. H., *An Introduction to the History of Wales*, Vol. I, 1941, Vol. II, 1948.

Williams, David, *A History of Modern Wales*, London, 1950.

Williams, David H., *The Welsh Cistercians*, Pontypool, 1969.

Williams, G. Haulfryn, *Railways in Gwynedd*, Caernarvon, 1979.

142

Index

144